Stefano Epifani

Digital Sustainability

Why **digital** transformation is the road to **sustainability**

2021

Author
Stefano Epifani

Series
Essays

Title
Digital Sustainability
why digital transformation is the road to sustainability

For further information and to contact the author
www.sostenibilitadigitale.it

Editor
Digital Transformation Institute
Via Ottaviano, 42
00192 Roma
www.digitaltransformationinstitute.it
info@digitaltransformationinstitute.it

Graphic Design
Fattoria Creativa s.r.l.
Director: Simone Pastorelli

Translator
Debora Bartolini

Cover Price
€. 24,00

ISBN
978-88-944841-5-1

Index

01.

Digital Transformation: the sense of a sense revolution

Where do we come from?

Valerio was torn away from the arms of Morpheus by the penetrating buzzing of the alarm on the bedside table. Just the time for a quick wash, he dressed up listening to the radio news to be aware of what was happening in the world: a young journalist must always keep updated. A quick breakfast while watching TV and then he was ready to hit the road, with the annoying beep-beep of his Casio fastened on his wrist, remembering him that it was time to hurry for the interview. Backpack on the shoulders, filled with his recording, his camera, and his faithful scratchpad. A pair of 60-minute cassettes and plenty of 36-shots camera rolls. Travel soundtrack from the Dire Straits' last album, Money for Nothing, using his brand new Walkman.

From the mention of Money for Nothing, the music lovers might have noticed that the previous passage is settled during the second half of the 80'. The Album, containing the namesake soundtrack, was issued over thirty years ago.

But even those who ignored the existence of The Dire Straits – pity for them – they would still be able with no effort to set the professional adventures of our young Valerio in that period.

It is the context of the instruments mentioned above which makes the time unmistakable: alarm clock, radio, wristwatch, camera and camera rolls, audiocassettes, and Walkman: these are landmark objects, marking the Golden Age of the analogic devices, before their inevitable waning.

When Mark Knopfler[1] strummed his Stratocaster for the first time to play Money for Nothing, the MS-DOS Operating-system had been released for two years, and Commodore had just started the production of Commodore 64. In conclusion: this is the turning point when computer science stops being just a science used by experts in lab coats, and computers enter all

[1] Mark Freuder Knopfler was the founder and leader of the rock band The Dire Straits, active from 1977 to 1995.

houses. It is the Age of "Personal Computer" (PC). This age has been developing over the last thirty years, laying the foundations for a radical change in our society. Nowadays, as it happened back in the 80' with analogic media, we are facing a new turning point.

Over time, indeed, digital logic came out of computers, where it was born, and entered all the objects. The process was slow but steady, implacable. After the first epical mainframe[2] and punch cards period, the first Pcs were fat, big boxes radiating heat like a gas stove, but they had far less computational skills than a modern gas stove would have nowadays (for the record, modern stoves are processed using the Internet and they decide automatically the room temperature, thanks to artificial intelligence systems far more complex than the machinery men used to go to the Moon.)

The first PCs had a precise purpose in a very precise space: usually an office desk. But things have changed over the years: the electronic components miniaturized, electrical expenditure decreased, and in the meantime, the battery autonomy of all the mobile-devices increased. And last but not least, the cost of the basic components dropped. Therefore, computer science became gradually suitable and useful – thanks to more and more powerful and cheap microchips – to control formerly analogic objects. The very same Java Language, which revolutionized computer science and which is well known among the digital experts, was created at first to control domestic appliances. Then the net developed – the Internet above all others – in order to link all these objects to one another and us as well.

The metamorphosis of the object started with the telephone. During the first decade of the new Millennium, the two distinct worlds of Computer science and Telecommunications fused, allowing the transformation of

[2] The word main frame (principal structure) refers to the first computers. They were real huge closets where the memories and processors were inserted in. At the end of the 70s' they were as big as rooms. Nowadays these very same closets contain computers made of miniature systems. Their computing and storage power is hundreds and thousands time better than it used to be in the past time.

the telephone, which shortly became the main front door to a highly connected and interactive world. All the tools mentioned in young Valerio's story – from the radio to television, from the Walkman to the camera, even the scratchpad – finally merged into one device: the telephone known as "smart" from now on.

The telephone became "smart" and changed in shape and functions, but this change affected its deepest meaning and purpose. Every single object bears within many different interactional dynamics in which the main players are: the customer, the object itself, and the surrounding environment. And in the specific case of a telephone, there is also another element: the system it gives access to. This can be a system with low complexity (another phone, used by Valerio to talk to his editor), or either a system with high complexity (for example, the Net, with its many languages and vastness.) The telephone underwent a significant change that affected either the functional components and above all, it redefined the customer interactions with the background and the systems it connects to. On these terms, the telephone's transformation into a smartphone was more than a mere functional enhancement; it was a real change in its purpose and role.

The smartphone – considered both as a device and as the material contact the customer has to a wider range of different changes – helped define a new way of communication and contributed to fully formulate the new paradigm of social interactions in its complexity. It did so by reshaping the interaction scheme of the customer with the services-system present in the Web and, thanks to simple and intuitive interfaces, it allowed the customer to be always online (no wonder we now talk about being always-on[3]).

If we had to retell Valerio's story in the present time, it would be completely different, starting from the counting of his instruments, to their usage in the light of the new technological experience.

[3] With the expression "always-on" we refer to the present condition of the internet users. Thanks to the widespread diffusion of the internet and of all the devices linked to it, they can be always connected to the internet. This condition produces a service-scheme based on the usage of the service itself in every moment and in every place.

As soon as he's awake, Valerio listens to the radio and watches TV, but now we do not use these instruments anymore. To get our information, we instead use social media, through which we talk to our contacts and – for better or for worse – we also get interesting news. This fact generated new behavioral patterns and new dynamics that still need to be analyzed and studied to fully comprehend their potential and even the possible risks that such a profound change could bring about.

Valerio needs a backpack to carry his tools – from the recorder to the camera, from the scratchpad to the Walkman – today, all these objects became one single device: the smartphone or the tablet. This union is not only a space-saver; it somewhat reshapes Valerio's interactional paradigm and also people's behavioral patterns. The Internet allows Valerio to work quickly (back in the day, the articles were even dictated on the phone, to the Newspaper's phototypesetter, for the following day), but though his work is quicker, it also bears a new meaning. Being a journalist, at present, is not just using faster devices. Still, it means a very different role in society, different from the time in which Mark Knopfler played Money for Nothing. The new-millennium-born Valerio shall have a very different social role, different from the 80'-born Valerio; he will be a journalist acting in a new social and economic background, highly influenced by the development of digital technologies.

These digital technologies changed people's way of thinking, how they get their information, how they choose (starting from the booking of a hotel for their holidays to their vote for the Elections), they established new ways to interplay with the device. Through the device, they also set new ways to interplay with other people and with a broader and broader service-ecosystem.

Thanks to these services, not only connected to the digital information, – in the Internet of Things[4] Age – the smartphone and many other objects

---

[4] With the expression Internet of Things, IoT, one refers to the internet connections linking potentially every object to the web, in full autonomy, without human intervention. These objects connect to the Web in order to communicate their Status and in order to supply data about their actions to other devices or to people, also to gather new data

now starting with the prefix "smart" (watches, glasses, even cars) became real interfaces with the surrounding reality. These devices are used to:

- Deal with other people;
- Grant access to all the available information on the Web;
- Enrich the interactions in a physical world made of objects connected to one another and us.

This concept of "smartness" can be explained as a middle way between "intelligence," "fastness," and "flexibility." Therefore, this concept is not merely linked to the single object but can be applied to an ecosystem-logic-dimension where the objects can interplay with each other. This ecosystem is (or wants to be) "smart" as a whole, thus reshaping the customer's experience.

One can talk about smart living, thinking about a new meaning for the concept of home, smart working, thinking about the effect on the working dimension; moreover, one can talk about smart cities, thinking about the urban dimension. And so on.

It is meaningless to try and distinguish the material from the virtual inside these logics and dimensions. At most, one could refer to two permeating dimensions of the same reality: a material one and a digital one.

Moreover, these dimensions keep changing, dynamically rewriting themselves, in relation to the human being, the core of this complex changing path. It changes developing opposite tensions and divergent forces; the result is what we now call "digital transformation."

---

and give cutting-edge services. The term was created in 1999 by the English engineer and scholar Kevin Ashton.

What do we mean by digital transformation?

A real struggle. Trying to persuade her father and uncle – the "founders" – to invest to be properly online had turned out to be more difficult than expected. She had heard anything. "There's no need." "We've always been doing like this." "Now, it's not the right time to invest." "What does the internet have to do with cheese?" Actually, she had answered convincingly, but her answers only generated more questions. Anna was deeply exasperated. But she knew somehow she mustn't give up. She couldn't just leave the company to the Fax Era. She always heard talking about the Internet, e-commerce, digital transformation. To tell the truth, she was not so sure she knew exactly what this transformation was all about… After all, she was educated at the Agricultural Institution: about cheese, she could deliver a lecture. She was pretty much born in it! But the internet, computers, technology, she had always shown little interest. Like those little truffle caciottas, everybody knows it is just an artificial flavor, a fake. Large-scale retail for tourists—another story. Nothing to do with the freshly cut hay she loved so much. Nevertheless, she sensed that behind all those meaningless big words, there was something noteworthy. Something that could change her company for the best. Or something that could cause a lot of problems…

If one had to make a chart for the most misunderstood terms, "digital transformation" would be top of the list. Anna's dismay is more than legitimate. The term "digital transformation" is now commonly widespread. However, as it often happens with new words and neologisms connected to the Information & Communication Technology (ICT) Branch, confusion on the real meaning of such terms can lead to misinterpretation. The deep meaning of the phenomenon they ought to describe is thus misunderstood.

The causes of this endemic term confusion in the digital world are different. On the one hand, every time there is a new trend or a new phenomenon, there is the flawed need – humanly understandable after all – to coin more and more original words. On the other hand, business marketing dealing with technology, consulting, and innovation and its tendency to always coin new words in order to sell new services and new products, not so brand new, truth to be told. It is a real chase after modern technology, useful to enrich the suppliers' finances, and cast a gloom over the customers. As a result, companies are driven away from the real innovation, they have it thrown in the face when the time is not ripe, and they are made to believe it is outdated when actually they should be ready to embrace it. This necessity to offer more and more trendy technology only benefits the income of the suppliers.

The very notion of digital transformation ended up in this general chaos. The term digital transformation is often mixed up and confused with the term digitization. Mixing these two terms up is like a synecdoche, a section for the whole. When talking about the word digitization, the focus is on the technological aspect and the procedure aspect. The term Digital transformation brings attention also to the economic, psychological, and social impact of this change. Furthermore, mixing these two concepts in Business Marketing – our poor Anna, to clarify – is misleading. One could think that digitizing their own companies is the only action to be taken, but one has to deal above all with the issues connected to the digital transformation. And that is a different story.

What are, therefore, the main differences between these two concepts? What do we mean by digital transformation, why is this phenomenon so important, and how will it affect people, the economy, and society?

Originally there was digitization, the process dimension

Imagine a lecture hall full of Millennials[5], imagine to ask them the question, "what does the word information science mean?". The reaction, incredible as it may seem, to such a simple question would be unexpected. Some hands would rise, of course, but most of them would look away,

[5] With the word Millennial we refer to people born between 1981 and 1996. These young people, grown up during the spread of the digital technologies, have been deeply affected by them on cultural, personal, professional and commercial grounds. [source: M.Dimock, *Defining generations: Where Millennials end and Generation Z begins, Pew Research Center*, 17 January 2019]

tripped up in a definition that is often taken for granted but actually shouldn't. The situation gets worse if one should ask the definition of "web" or the difference between "internet" and "intranet." Moreover, what the hell is that strange acronym[6] followed by a double slash, appearing on every website address? Footnote: an audience of businessmen, public officers, or white-collars would react just the same to those questions. Or even worse.

It is no wonder if our human capital deserves one of the worst international rating positions[7] about technological skills.

People often do not realize that some concepts are complicated (at different levels) and abstract, even if they are commonly used. We take them for granted, but they are not. Even the German poet Goethe wrote: "there is nothing more difficult to spot, that what you have just under your nose." The result is that people often ignore the basics. However, most of these basic concepts – consider, for example, "information science" or "internet," to mention the easiest ones – are not axiomatic. It is not easy to fully understand their essence if one ignores their meaning.

To fully understand what we mean by digital transformation, we need to start from the beginning, from the concept of "information science" itself. Everyone knows or at least should know that the concept of information science comes from the expression "automatic information[8]." Therefore,

---

[6] HTTP is the acronym for "HyperText Transfer Protocol" and shows the protocol through which the information is sent on the web. It has been developed at CERN, in Geneve by a research team, Tim Berners-Lee amongst them is thus considered the "father" of the web. Together with the other acronyms HTML (HyperText Markup Language) and URLs (Uniform Resource Locator) they create the information technology core of the World Wide Web (WWW).

[7] Italy is in the last positions on every international rating, measuring Countries innovation levels. For example, the DESI (Digital Economy and Society Index): in 2019 Italy places itself in the 24thposition out of 28 EU States, for the fourth year in a row. [Source: Digital Economy and Society Index (DESI), national Report for 2019]

[8] Translator's note: In Italian, the word Information Science is rendered with the term *Informatica* and originates from the contraction of the two terms information and automatic.

information science deals with the automation of every information process. Of course, these information processes need to be compatible with computers' language: the binary system. It is based on digital logic, a logic able to code the information using binary numbers, the only numbers – up to now – computers can understand. The binary number system is based on the bit (binary number), assuming two values: 0 and 1. Digitizing all the information means, therefore, to code it using the binary model – in other words, it means to rewrite it through a series of 0s and 1s –to be processed in an automated way by a calculator that, fast as it can be, can only read these two digits.

That is that. Basically, digitization is: translating the processes using a digital language to deal with them in an automated manner. Whether the process is (apparently) easy, the results it brings about are not.

It is clear, for example, that the transition from an analogic approach to a digital logic gives the chance to rethink the process. This process loses thus its analogic and material dimension and becomes an algorithm that can lead to a better efficiency/effectiveness relation.

To go beyond, we can state that digitization is about how we make things. Its dimension process is about "how" people or companies run their activities. In other words, thanks to digitization and technology, the processes can be highly enhanced. Sometimes the changes brought about by digitization can be marginal, but sometimes the processes can be completely revolutionized. Suffice to say, for example, the research activity in a library or a catalog: the physical limit of material devices used to store the data in the analogic era led to the creation of complex systems for cataloging. Inside a library, all the data about books are divided into aisles; aisles can be divided by historical period, style, author, etc. Finding information about a text preserved in a library is not so simple. Since we have to obey the physical limit imposed by the analogic structures in which it is kept. Windows Operating System uses the very same metaphor, based on windows and folders. It proposes physical boundaries, completely unnecessary in a digital contest, but this metaphor had helped hundreds of people to get to know an abstract concept, otherwise free of any heuristic connections. Switching from analogic information to digital information, today, we just have to digit a keyword in the search bar, and the web browser will immediately present all the hits connected to that word. All the "limits" of the analogic world are gone. We can redefine and engineer a process – the research process, in this case – using the true potential of the digital world. However, the focus is on how we act and not on the result of the action.

To sum up:

- **The real change is on the "how"**. When we talk about process digitization, even if the action itself entails a formal change in the process, we have to remember that it does not change the purpose and the final goal. In other words, whether we use the taxonomic system, typical of all the bibliographic catalogs, or a keyword-based system, typical of all the search engines, the purpose of our action does not change. The only thing that changes is how.
- **It is a choice**. Digitization is and always will be a choice made by people or by the organization. Maybe for companies, it is a choice compelled by Trade and by contingency; for individuals, it is compelled by interpersonal relationships and contacts. But it will always be a choice. No one will arrive and force the corporate manager to use e-mails instead of faxes. No one will be obliged to use a computer to write a report, rather than a typewriter or a pen and inkbottle. Epicure used to say that no one chooses evil willingly. Still, they are stuck in this evil if they think it is better than another evil: so we need to understand – with digitization – what the greater evil is.

Suppose we had to look at Valerio and Anna's perspective. That is to say, if we had to imagine the impact of digitization on jobs (the young journalist Valerio) and companies (like Anna, our agricultural businesswoman), we should think about all the different changes in the technological context of the last decades, and how these changes affected these different situations. It's been ages since when using a typewriter was all you needed to do to be a journalist. Nowadays, the media scenario evolved. Today, Valerio must know all the social media; he must be able to tell the difference between a reliable source and fake news, he must find his way in the maze of archives, full of data, useful to understand the reality (but actually, how many journalists can use data journalism?), he must know video and audio post-production software. And even more. The same goes for Anna. She has to learn how to use project management software; she has to communicate with public administration using digital channels (designed to make life easier, but sometimes considered a burden by business people). She needs to understand the better way of communication with her customers employing these new channels. And so on.

And then came digital transformation: the sense dimension

Digitalization refers to all those actions enhancing the processes, through the automation and re-engineering, made possible thanks to Information science. But what is going to happen when information science becomes pervasive? What is going to happen when computer diffusion overflows exponentially, and computers enter all houses? Furthermore, what is going to happen when the development of the Internet ("The Web"), the inception of social media, and the widespread availability of smart devices (first of all smartphones) allow people to connect to the web services from every device, in every place and every moment, making computers practically useless? What will happen when digital interaction becomes so pervasive to affect people's behaviors, the way they communicate, they get their information, form an opinion, reshape their event horizon, buy things, meet new people, make friends, do business, fall in love? What will happen when personal relationships become a function deeply related to technologies and social networks? What will happen when it becomes more and more difficult to distinguish between traditional interpersonal moments and those determined by a technological process?

That is the transition – among other things – from the digitization to the digital transformation dimension. The presence of digital technologies in this dimension is profoundly affecting people's behaviors, relational schemes, interactional dynamics, generating a relentless individual and collective behavioral remediation[9] process. In its turn, this process brings about a real change of perception in many different aspects of our society.

The overflow of digital interactions generates a radical change in people's behavior and their values lever. In other words, this changed scenario deeply affects people and society's inner motivation, developing a transformative dimension. This dimension sees the digital world as a catalyst, causing a transformation in people and society. So, digital transformation affects not only the processes but also perceptions: it has the power to change the perception of things because it affects the choice engines. A real perception revolution, based on the different feelings of the concept of value (applied to all the various aspects: interpersonal relationship value, institutional value, goods and services values, information value, and even people's value) producing a profound change in every part of life.

So digital transformation gives Valerio new and more powerful tools to carry out his job. Above all, it rewrites the definition of journalist completely, giving him a new role and placing him in a new dimension in society. The Web allows not only the enhancement of the work processes used to print a journal but also redefines the perception of a journalist, imposes the new rules of the job, and molds a new professional figure whose job will be to deal with new contexts and also to deal with his new role in society. The same goes for Anna. She needs to enhance her company, thanks to technologies. Still, she also needs to find a new business scheme, based on her customers – who use social media, get their information online, and look for new experiences – they have already changed. They have integrated with the dynamic developed in the market by digital transformation. By changing the parameters used to explain reality, we also change value and choice leverage. It is fundamental for Anna to monitor and understand this to enhance her company.

---

[9] The term "remediation" is a loan from J. Bolter and R. Grusin. In their work Remediation: understanding New Media, 2003, they describe the impact of the "new media" in the medial ecosystem as a whole.

Thus, if digitization is a mere choice made by the firm, a redefinition of procedures (what we can call a "how" dimension), digital transformation – in its dimension of perception revolution – refers to the "what" dimension. It affects the way we do things, but above all, it redefines the sense. Digitization allows us to make things better, but digital transformation rewrites what is sensible to do.

Considering this dynamic, digitization deals with the way we do things, digital transformation deals with the sense of things. Technologies always bring about a sense of change in some social and marketing contexts. Before the spread of watches and alarm clocks, in many English towns, for example, there was the so-called warner. He used to knock to people's windows with a long stick – mainly to laborers' windows because they had to wake before dawn to go to work – and warned them it was time to wake up. The spreading of alarm clocks made this profession useless, changing the customers' value scales so that they did not consider such activity useful anymore. A technological enhancement of all his practical tools wouldn't have changed a thing. Neither the streamlining of the operating processes would have made the difference. Lighter sticks or graphene sticks (now it's trendy) wouldn't have saved this activity from extinction, nor using expedited itineraries. In the same way, digital transformation operates on the perception of things, on the perception of the value they have for people, on the value lines of companies themselves. It is not just a mere change in how we do things, but it is instead a redefinition of what is sensible and what, in a transformed scenario, is useless.

To sum up:

- **The change is on the "what".** What's the point of being the most reliable warner in town if the town doesn't need a warner anymore? The need for warners is not a result of their being good or bad in their job, but either it depends on how the evolution of technology, society, and trade affects such a job's utility. Technology has always been both a tool and an active player, causing transformation processes, but the digital is a real catalyst. It produced a sprint process in the redefinition of perception, involving all the social classes, all the industries, all the professions, using its leverage to develop converging trans-medial[10] processes, concerning communication and the meeting between information technology and operational technology[11], concerning services and industrial processes. For better or for worse, today, every field, every branch has been affected by digital transformation. Today, every social and economic area needs to ask about the change led by technologies seen as instruments to remediate perception. It means that every field must ask itself what it is sensible to do in a world where people's values change according to digital transformation dynamics. If digitization changes the way we do things, digital transformation redefines what makes sense.

- **It is a condition**. If digitization is a choice, digital transformation is a condition. Digital transformation is a process concerning society as a whole, not only a single individual or a single organization (even though every individual and every organization must acknowledge how to interact with it). Pertaining to the range of deep social motivations, it deals with the way society rewrites itself in a kaleidoscope. On one side, technology as a developing engine; on the other side, people as real players of this development. Single individuals and single companies can only choose to study and understand this collective change's direction and maybe take part in co-defining it. They cannot stop it, though. And by ignoring it, they cannot ignore its results. If our warner hadn't come to terms with the fact that his abilities were of no

---

[10] With the expression trans-medial we mean the content distribution by means of different medias, and its enrichment on the base of the specific features of the single media. This term is the foundation of the concept of "transmedia storytelling", postulated by the American Henry Jenkins. It is seen as a narrative form developing through different media, enriching the customer's experience. [source: H. Jenkins Convergence Culture, 2007]

[11] With the expression Operational Technology (OT) we mean the total of the hardware and software tools detecting the status and/or activating operations able to automatize and optimize the processes, thanks to the monitoring and the control they have over industrial machineries, goods, processes and unexpected events. They are essential for the monitoring and safekeeping of the systems and of the crucial infrastructure such as energy systems and water systems. At first they were considered opposite to the Information Technologies, but today, thanks to the IoT they seem to merge with them. [source: Gartner]

use anymore, he would have been condemned by the progressing of alarm clocks in every house. The same places he used to knock at with his stick. He couldn't help stop the spread of alarm clocks. The digital transformation pervades society and helps rewrite the rules, models, and boundaries: following this rhythm of change and trying and defining it is the only possible option not to be knocked over.

Digital transformation and innovation

Digital transformation is not digitization. That is verified. But what about the concept of innovation? What is the relationship between innovation, digital transformation, and digitization? Threesomes are really difficult to deal with, and this threesome makes no exception. In this case, as well, innovation and digital transformation are easily mixed up, dealing with innovation as a specific type of digital transformation, giving it inexact connotation and significance.

To start with: what is innovation?

It is not easy to define innovation. It is no easy because, due to its inner multidimensionality and its semantic ambiguity, it is actually a deeply polysemous concept. Furthermore, this concept is so vast it can be used and adapted to many different interpretations according to the context. For the last two centuries, the need to find a proper definition has been challenging scholars worldwide.
There are also studies to try and find a suitable definition of the concept of innovation. One of these studies made a list of almost one hundred different definitions[12], to quote the more widespread only.

Back when no one would have imagined, when the Internet and digital transformation had yet to come, Joseph Schumpeter described innovation as "creative destruction[13]." With its disruptive force, it could compel society to evolve or extinguish in terms of market economy. Back in the

[12] A. Baregheh, J. Rowley, S. Sambrook, Towards a multidisciplinary definition of Innovation, Management decision 47.8 (2009): 1323-1339.
[13] J. A. Schumpeter, Capitalism, Socialism and Democracy. ETAS, 2001.

'40s of the last century, people didn't talk about digital, for sure, but innovation was felt as inevitable, and also its potential impacts, for better or for worse. Schumpeter's statement applies well to the outcomes of modern technologies such as the Internet, artificial intelligence, or robotics – to name some – on our society.

These outcomes brought about a profound reconsideration of nature, rules, and society's very processes, bringing along consequences, not always good. Nonetheless, they force the civil gathering to face lacerating changes, going beyond a technological determinism. It is not wrong to consider it naïve but should be too optimistic to think it outdated.
These changes are not a "side effect" of innovation but an inherent feature. This feature needs to be understood because it becomes the development-lever, and we have to set the direction of such development. In this direction, the social results of the digital technology impacts – being today the most potent innovation driver we have at our disposal – are so crucial because they involve every aspect of society in a sense dimension (think about work, privacy, freedom, relationships, information, trade).

Therefore, it is fundamental to understand the dynamics of innovation to use it as a development lever and be able to rule the variables and create positive impacts. Always aware that the adverse outcomes linked to changes are not so easy to cancel.
That is the reason why it is so important to evaluate the innovation processes and, in the meantime, to set the goals scrupulously, whether they are companies' business goals or a Country's. Or even those of the World we live in.
It is not a case that an organization like the OECD (Organization for Economic Co-operation and Development) has been devoting the last 20 years to the definition of methods and structures of innovation. It has issued a survey, updated continuously[14], in the previous edition – referring explicitly to Schumpeter's work – it defines four different types of innovation[15]:

---

[14] We refer to the Oslo Manual, issued in first edition in 1992. The last edition was issued in 2018.
[15] Oslo Manual, Guidelines for Collecting and Interpreting Innovation Data, OECD, 2018.

- **Product innovation**: it applies to all those goods and services, new or significantly improved; it means developing the production techniques, the materials, and components, the software, the management of the User Interface, and other functional features. The moment Anna crafts a new type of mozzarella cheese and decides to place it in the market, she develops a process of product innovation.
- **Process innovation:** it applies to production and development systems, new or extensively improved. It means significant changes in production techniques, in the machinery, or management software. The moment Valerio stops using his old Olivetti Typewriter to write his articles and starts using a PC, or again, the moment he forwards an email, instead of dictating his article on the phone, he is innovating a section of the journal's innovation process.
- **Marketing innovation:** it applies to the new marketing techniques, to the new channels to reach the customer, to the design, the packaging of the product, the pricing, and the channels of communication. The moment Anna stops sending postal marketing catalogs and opens a page on the most ordinary social network sites and starts interacting with them using this channel, she develops a marketing innovation.
- **Organizational innovation:** it applies to the new organizational models and also to the management of human resources and foreign relationships. When Valerio's newsroom puts together information and production processes, using the radio and the press resources as a whole, making no difference between the radio and the journal editing, it is operating an organizational innovation.

Whether it is a product, process, marketing, or organizational innovation, there are basically only two types of innovation: sustaining innovation and disruptive innovation. The expression sustaining innovation stresses that ongoing improving process, typical of all changes, especially in traditional firms and consolidated markets. This phenomenon allows products and organizations to deal with little but steady changes.

However, 30 years ago, Clayton Christensen and Joseph Bower[16] had already noticed the important novelty these new technologies brought about: innovation, until then continuative and steady, would have become radical, with disruptive results on markets, products, and people. The digital contributed only to magnify this phenomenon.

And what about the threesome?

Innovation and digitalization are – to quote Facebook – in a complicated relationship. Even more complicated if we include digital transformation factor. These three elements are tightly bounded, but for the sake of simplification, for the need of conceptualizing, or for mere ignorance, their cause-effect relation is too often reversed. Therefore, we need to look carefully at the vertexes of this triangle and their interdependence because some of the most important phenomena in our society are ascribed to its perimeter.

Schumpeter talks explicitly about products, processes, organizational and market innovation: technological innovation is not on his list. Not because it is not essential, instead because it is transversal to all of the others.

Innovation is not only technological, but every innovation is based on technology.

From the discovery of fire to the wheel invention, from the movable type printing technology to the steam engine, from the microchip to the computer network, from Artificial Intelligence to the *blockchain*, these standard changings have always been determined by technological elements that nurtured progress and human development.

Today technology is mostly digital technology. We have been living in the so-called fourth industrial revolution era[17]. The rules and markets are redefined by applying computer technologies and logics to the industrial

[16] C. Christensen, J. Bower, Disruptive Technologies: catching the wave, Harvard Business Review, 1995.
[17] K. Schwab, The Fourth Industrial revolution, World Economic Forum, 2015

processes. Technology in general and digital technology, in particular, are the main instruments of innovation, which are put into action whenever the product or the service is on trade in the market[18] for the first time. We can talk about innovation whenever an invention (that is not an innovation by itself) is launched on the market.
How does digital transformation fit in this picture? Whether innovation, technology, and digitalization are all connected to one another by a cause-effect relationship (innovation is a result of the positive application of digital technology to a process, a product, or a service), digital transformation is the sense context in which innovation develops.

From this perspective, digital transformation is innovation's reference scenario: the context in which the social dimension determines innovation's and technological development's trajectories, reshaping people's needs, reshaping markets' features, setting social priorities and necessities.

Digital transformation is, first of all, a social phenomenon, taking its basis from digitization, but developing in a complex maze of connections between people, market, and society. Following new creation (and conception) models of value, this maze reshapes the modern world's scenarios, going beyond merely technological and economic dimensions. Through them, it redefines people's social relationships that reflect, like a game of mirrors, society, and economy, drawing new boundaries and new features.

Digital transformation results from digitalization, but it becomes more: it becomes both a scenario and a changing bearer. It affects both society and the development of technologies; it contributes to a living rewriting of social and human rules using technological remediation models. It is now fundamental to understand these models to acknowledge the development of our society.

---

[18] C. Freeman, The Economics of Industrial Innovation, Penguin Modern Economics Texts, 1974.

How do we react to innovation?

He had earned that bloody license. A mortgage for the next ten years. "it's worth it." He kept telling himself. Actually, he didn't have much choice: three children are expensive and also two marriages. Alfio knew the town like the back of his hand, and he had always loved driving. What about the occupational hazard? Of course. "I'm 6 feet tall and weigh 200 pounds; that should help!" he kept telling his friends. Wrongdoers didn't know that, actually, he was a kind soul. In conclusion, he would be indebted for a few years, but he would have lived a quiet life as a taxi driver.

A quiet life. Would it really be? Actually, it depends on the historical period we set the story. Because, if Alfio were a contemporary of the famous roman taxi driver ("tassinaro") Pietro Marchetti, a character played by the Italian actor Alberto Sordi[19], in the first years of the 80s' we wouldn't have a doubt. Marchetti, thanks to his cab, can lead a quiet life, his son goes to university (in New York), he goes on vacation, and he's happy with his life. But if Alfio were born in the '80s and took his license nowadays, he probably would have been unwise on a long-term perspective.

The reason is apparent: the new models of urban transportation now developing – from Uber to the sharing economy and the self-driving cars – even if opposed by administrations (and taxi drivers, of course) will lead to a new remodeling of the taxi driver as a job, changing the way we know it and wiping out, in the long run, licenses' commercial value.

Society, preservation, and change

History repeats itself. More than once, actually. But we never learn the lesson. Back in the second half of the XX Century, automobiles started spreading in England and the US, hindering – according to the majority

[19] The tassinaro (taxi driver) is a comedy by and with Alberto Sordi, famous roman actor and director, active from the early 40s' until 2001. He died in 2003.

– the railway service and above all the urban carriage transportation. Carriages pulled by horses, to be precise. A breakthrough like an automobile boded (ill or well, according to the different points of view) to mark an unprecedented change of scheme. This change jeopardized many different roles at that time: railway business people and coachmen, to name a few.

We can try to figure out their reaction; they would have tried to understand the world's change in the light of this new invention, to understand the impact on their activities and – consequently – how to react. It is too easy to look at history in hindsight: someone used to say that our biggest problem is living our own life looking in one direction and understand it by staring from the opposite. In this perspective, those men's effort, threatened by the spread of automobiles, was to stop the world from changing, rather than figure out how the world would have changed thanks to cars. So they perpetrated a lobbying action that led to the issue of the "Red Flag Act." A set of rules forcing people who wanted to travel to town not to exceed the speed limit of 2 miles per hour and to drive behind a "warner," waving a red flag, warning people of the "forthcoming danger." This solution sounds hilarious to us. It is like trying to catch smoke with your bare hands. At that time, it seemed the best solution to try and stop the dire consequences of innovation.

Today is no different. Some particular categories see emerging technologies as a potential threat to their existence – or the keeping of their status – and they try to stop the advancing of the enemy, usually technology, innovation, and progress, by issuing new laws that should procrastinate the damage.

When dealing with individuals, organizations, or different expressions of society, human behavior – like those of every living being – is always conservative. Once they have found a balance, built a "comfort zone," they tend to keep it and preserve it as long as possible. Whether it is for fear of change or to keep a power position, every complex system fights a lost battle between the rising entropy and the struggle to bring order. This challenge is the juxtaposition between the established order and the innovation generating change – the invention that finds its application –

and in this challenge, the breaking element compels the dynamic redefinition of the leverage. This reaction is understandable, human, acceptable even. Still, it is useless because it is doomed to clash with the inevitable, and it is also evil because it hinders looking at problems in the right perspective.

The inversion of cause and effect

This reaction is entirely understandable. But the attempts to stop an inexorable change are fallacious; we can try at least to determine its direction.

So far, dozens of industrial sectors have been remolded by digital transformation. The main actors of the industrial sector, in most cases, weren't the leaders of the change: they were instead the victims.

Like always, history sets the example. Think about the music sector: in the '90s, people used to think that the main reason for the sales crisis in the music industry was piracy. So, while every record company spent time and money trying to stop this process, a computer-selling company appeared and proved that piracy was a fake problem. Apple and its iTunes had great merit in rethinking the whole sector. It started focusing on the user's needs and the dynamics of the context, not on the product's consolidated features at that time. Apple focused on music buyers and acknowledged that, in a digital market, a product like the Compact Disk (CD) was pointless. Soundtracks could be sold individually and, above all, online. Thus, they developed an aggressive trading policy, so well-structured that all the other majors had but one choice: to join. What was the outcome? For a long time, Apple was the biggest record company globally (now its ruling position has been undermined by another firm, Spotify, not in the music industry. This is like a reminder to tell us that in this area, even the most solid monopoly lasts shortly). But above all, record companies were forced to play a supporting role in their own sector, invaded by other actors from the digital world.

Record companies made a double mistake. On the one hand, they believed their market was stable and their product immutable, and users' logic always the same. On the other, they felt the reason for the crisis of the music market was piracy. Instead, piracy was just the symptom of the wrong alignment between the supply of the product and the customers' demand. This was a real inversion of cause and effect.

The result was to leave ample space of maneuver to an operator coming from the digital world, and thus it did not consider the product unchangeable and did not consider the distribution channel as consolidated, but considered them both to be a corollary of the user. The user was the focus, around whom to redefine the strategy and the sector's whole sequence value.

Whether we are dealing with music (for example, Apple and Spotify), video (YouTube and Netflix), travels (Booking), relationships (the complex ecosystem of Facebook and Instagram), food service (who's never used Tripadvisor or The Fork?), commerce (Amazon and Alibaba), currency (like bitcoin and its epigones) and more. Innovation, applied in the digital transformation era, operates like this: it redefines the meaning of entire market sectors according to customers' needs and behavior, coping with the data they are creating and dealing with pre-existing market data to reformulate the value's production chains. With the expression Platform Economy, we mean the crucial role of those actors managing the users, the markets, and the transactions between them thanks to platforms' use. These platforms are more and more critical for the economy. But there's something more. There is a process of creative destruction – to quote Schumpeter – bringing about a relentless redefinition of sense for the markets and consequently for society. It is fundamental to understand these dynamics to determine the directions and answer the only sensible question: which society do we choose to live in?

Towards a holistic approach of innovation

Even though Schumpeter's considerations were on a large-scale and examined innovation as a social-changing engine, it is clear how his focus, in modeling the concept, was on the economic dimension of the phenomenon, as a means of development and change.

However, recently, we started to understand how innovation is not merely connected to economic growth but can be read as social development lever. Looking systematically at innovation as a means of change focused on improving society is the cause that led sociologists, technicians, and economists to talk about "social innovation."

"Back in the Eighties and Nineties, the concept of innovation was addressed to firms. Once, economic and social matters were considered as separate. The economy produced wealth, social matters were expensive. In the 21st Century, that is not true anymore. Sectors such as health, social services, or education are growing, and they are a wide part of Countries' GDP, and they create jobs, while other sectors are still in crisis. In the long run, innovation in social and education sectors will be as important as in the pharmaceutical industry and aerospace industry[20]." That was the opening passage of Guide to Social Innovation issued by the European Commission to test the matter's importance and its role as a change engine.

Innovation thus can be described – quoting Schumpeter and describing the effects in a broader dimension, from a single company to society as a whole – like the development and implementation of new ideas, products, services, and models, fulfilling needs and creating new social relationships aimed to improve social welfare. It aims to the improvement of human welfare rather than economic growth. Social innovations are social both in their purposes and their meanings. These innovations bring about social welfare, on the one hand, and they improve the social acting skills of the individuals living in society, on the other[21].

This change's direction can only be determined by forcing society to face clear goals and specific challenges. These challenges are well explained in the 17 Sustainable Development Goals issued by the United Nations, a blueprint to fulfill up to 2030.

---

[20] Diogo Vasconcelos (1968-2011), Chairman of SiX (Social Innovation eXchange).

[21] Adaptation from Guide to Social Innovation. DG Regional and Urban Policies, 2013.

In this particular historical period, the majority still reckons innovation as an economic growth lever; that is why Nations' political agenda must be set on innovation as a means of social and economic sustainability, in full compliance with the environment, according to new and more complex models. These models bear a new approach towards innovation, digitization, and digital transformation; it is fundamental, then, to understand the relations between these elements.

What future in digital transformation?

Alfio's problem with his license can be different according to perspective.

From the individual's point of view, earning a license now could mean a market price reduction in a few years. Every taxi driver faces this high risk; it is no coincidence that they are opposing any change.
The individual's point of view is understandable: the worker – whether a taxi driver, a doctor, a journalist, a blue-collar – he doesn't deal with economic politics nor with development politics. His goal is to support his family and himself.

What happens if we face the problem like society as its whole? What are institutions supposed to do in this complicated context? Of course, there are many answers to these questions, and there is no right or wrong.

Indeed, there are different possible approaches. The most common approach is the one used in last-of-XX-Century England with coachmen and the Red Flag Act. When in doubt, the problem is solved with a law. In the here and now, the law satisfies the stakeholders, brings consent, and – if in the right moment – even some votes. It is the easiest path: and it goes for public transportation, for the sharing economy, for riders, and copyright. Like always, the easiest way is not the most effective.

A law created to "forbid" a phenomenon resulting from a global evolutionary process only procrastinates the problem, postpones the outcomes, and slackens the development. As a result, the impact is usually even more devastating when the ineffective regulatory bulwark eventually falls.

It does not mean that Alfio is to be left at the mercy of the digital transformation, and his profession wiped out in the name of an undefined "progress."

The problem is more complicated than it seems at first. And often politicians – from every political Party – just give it a quick glimpse.

On the one hand, politicians need to safeguard the actors, their job, their sector, and above all their stability, at risk because of digital transformation. On the other hand, they must develop appropriate economic policies to slow down the development of innovation. In such a globalized context, it would lead to negative outcomes for the country if that should happen.

Therefore, institutions have a double role: whether promoting innovation is essential, it is also necessary to safeguard all those categories struck by the negative impacts. It means they need to define methods and systems, and even governance policies and formulas. Thanks to these formulae, a part of the economic wealth generated by innovation should be used to help those who, on the other hand, are endangered by innovation itself—a sort of subsidiarity, balancing the pros and cons of digital transformation.

The solution, as simple as it may seem, is not given for granted. History teaches: there are two main approaches to deal with the problem, but neither follow this setting:

- **The market approach** (a few laws, only to promote innovation), to encourage innovation, does not consider the adverse outcomes, believing that the market itself would solve the problem. The United States are the champions of this approach. But now that the Silicon Valley boom's initial euphoria is gone, they understand that not all that glitters is gold.
- **The dirigiste approach** (legislate, and when in doubt, forbid) tries to limit the potential damages of innovation and misses the advantages. The final result is, however, negative. The European Union is the example, and for it, nothing glitters, not even gold!

42[22]

It does not seem to be the right solution for poor Alfio. At least, he is not alone. Alfio, Anna, Valerio. They are in the same boat, after all. We all are. The taxi driver, the farmer, the journalist. Retailers, artisans, freelancers. But also business people, white-collars, blue-collars, and doctors.

The whole world is facing a radical change, and technologies are the real catalysts, triggering a changing process of which we know the departure point but not the destination. Too often, we acknowledge the change when it has already happened, and as a result – not at all secondary – we cannot con-determinate it.

To gather the signals of this change and more, to be proactive and engaged to turn this change into positive, we need two elements, at least:

1. **Good knowledge of the new technologies shaping our world.** It does not mean that we need to be technicians, but certainly, we need to be more technologists. It means to be able, no matter our job, to read all the dynamics, subtended to the different technologies to understand the impacts on the market and society. The interdisciplinary dimension is thus fundamental: recent history showed that the knowledge of the dynamics of Information Technology and the knowledge of digital transformation directions have been even more crucial than understanding the product markets interested by change. At what cost? What is the result in terms of global welfare? To optimize the positive impacts of digital transformation and marginalize the side effects, it is necessary to read the different sectors and explain the change provoked by digitization, adjusting the knowledge of the technological and digital dynamics and the contexts where these dynamics are declined.
2. **Know the direction to take.** That is even more complicated than deciphering technologies and declining their impacts on the market and society. At this stage, the development and economic models, given for granted, cannot cope with this world's com-

[22] This title is for a selected few... all other people, please read footnote number 22.

plexity, which, using concepts such as speed, growth, and connection like mantras, did not waste time defining their true meaning. Now, these mantras are transforming the face of our society. But how?

From the combination of these two points, the capacity to interpret the technologies and the capacity to show the path of their development, the core of the problem arises: interpreting the digital transformation to direct the impacts for the creation of a sustainable society.

For a long time, too long – according to the digital world's time – the focus of experts, scholars, economists, and philosophers was on asking whether the technology was good or bad.

- Does artificial Intelligence create or destroy jobs?
- Does the *blockchain* simplify or complicate economic exchanges?
- Is robotics going to improve people's working condition or is going to enslave people?
- Are big data going to contribute to building a knowledge society, or are we going to be the victims of big data administrators?
- Is the Internet of things going to have a positive impact on security ground, or is it going to develop a society of control?
- Are social networks able to open new communication channels, or are they going to prevent us from real communication?
- Does virtual reality go beyond physical limits giving us new possibilities, or does it make us estranged from the world?

We could go on and on, merely reporting questions, objects of important reflections and meetings, the inspiration for books, essays, dissertations, research papers. The problem is the so-called Cognitive Tunneling[23], as

[23] With the expression "Cognitive Tunneling", also known as "inattentional blindness" we refer to people's tendency – once placed in a context – not to notice or take into consideration everything that is outside the scheme of that given context. That is why, when posing a question, the semantic scheme of that question creates a particular set of answers. If the question is set on the base of a precise model (ex. Are technologies good or bad?) all the answers will be oriented on the base of that model, ignoring all the other possible models (ex. How can technologies be developed in order to be good for society?)

Douglas Adams[24] used to say, we asked the wrong questions. As a result, from this mistake, it wasn't possible to get the answers we needed. On the contrary, we procrastinated the finding of solutions.

The digital role has been considered in a determinist manner, but depicting it in society to control the outcomes would have meant to create an instrument for the fulfillment of precise goals, not a context element to understand in its good and bad implications.

We always say that technologies are not good nor bad; they are simply instruments that can be used in a good or bad way. But we have to bear in mind that we use these technologies – as single individuals or as a society – and therefore, technologies are neither good nor bad nor the way they are used.

Good and evil are in the vision of the society we decide to embrace. Technologies must be the acting instrument of a vision, a model, a project.

Looking at technologies as necessary instruments to build a better society is the only way to disentangle from the impasse of the last few years. Every argument about digital transformation has become so complicated that becoming the victims of technological determinism would be not a risk but a certainty.

We need to rethink the questions:

- The question is not whether artificial intelligence creates or destroys jobs; the question is how to use artificial intelligence to create a more sustainable job.
- The question is not whether the *blockchain* is a risk for the financial system, but how to get the chance of a great re-brokering.
- The question is not whether robotics will improve people's working conditions or is going to enslave people, but how to create

[24] In The Hitchhiker's Guide to the Galaxy, famous novel by the writer Douglas Adams (1979), mankind asks an Artificial Intelligence called Deep Thought the answer to "life, universe, and everything". After millions of years, Deep Thought finally answers the question: 42. "I checked carefully", said the computer "and that is surely the answer. To be honest, I think the problem is, you never knew what the question was."

systems able to lighten work, in those aspects otherwise stressful and unsustainable.

- The question is not whether big data will make us all victims of the social platforms, but how to use big data to improve the service system for the customer, protecting the right of privacy, with a new definition of ownership of data.
- The question is not how to stop the Internet of things from developing a society of control, but how to get free from the necessity of control
- The question is not whether we have been made incapable of communicating outside social networks, but how reality is changing in the face of this new context where digital and analogic communications weave together, developing new relationship models.
- The question is not whether virtual reality makes us estranged from the world, but how to act to make it an integration instrument.

And so on, trying to replace the wrong questions with the right ones and trying hard to find the answers.

And that is the problem.

To find the right answers, we need to:

1. Have clear in mind the kind of society we want to live in;
2. Know the direction we have to take to build it;
3. Understand how technologies can help us do it.

It is clear then that technologies are not the main problem; the problem is our vision of the future.

02.
Can we choose our future?

The future, is it a choice?

It was at dusk on an end-of-summer day. Valerio was looking at the waves crashing on the shore from his terrace while the wind was ruffling his white hair. Dusk always led him to reflect, but his reflections had changed over the last few years. As a young man, his thoughts were for the future. But now, he often got lost in his memories.

He used to remember his first steps as a journalist—the last years of the previous century. Newspapers were made of paper—the same for everyone. A bitter smile crossed his wrinkled face when he thought that real people wrote them. It has been a long time since he had retired from his job, or what was left of it. Retirement had revealed a shelter from this change; at the beginning, he had felt enthusiastic, then cold, and then suspicious. Adverse, at last. Coldness, diffidence, aversion. "Young people" used to tell him that it is how things go; it is the progress. He had to look beyond; he had to fit in, seize the change. He just couldn't come to terms with the fact that he didn't have to write his article personally but insert the data into his virtual assistant and supervise the results. The papers were clear, readable, no doubt. Some of his colleagues couldn't say the same; they couldn't afford a virtual assistant and still had to write their articles independently. Then all those local newspapers closed: readers didn't want standard pieces anymore. They wanted customized articles built on the reader's profile; they were a must. All those publishers who couldn't afford expensive artificial intelligence were out of the market. Pity. A lot of valuable journalists had to change their job. Others had to change when people got used to real-time videos, a journalist had no time to check their articles, but artificial intelligence never make mistakes. The avatars, then, were so good in declaiming them that human supervision was unnecessary. "Bio-journalists" (they were called like this to sort them from the artificial intelligence) were a few; they only had to operate the parameters for the definition of the journal editorial line. He had become the chief editor for a long time now, and his editorial staff was quick and efficient, but really quiet because when machines talk to each other, they are not so loud. And he, quietly, decided to quit.

The same gloomy silence of that end-of-summer sunset. He took a moment to understand what was wrong. He took a moment to realize what was the difference between the sunsets he remembered as a boy and this one. The seagulls. They were gone. No one would have believed that. No one had done anything to prevent it. The fact is that now they were not there to chirp to the ships, coming back with their fish shipment. The truth is, no ships were coming back, simply because there were no fish left. Plastics had killed them off, at last. And seagulls as well, so they had disappeared from the shores. The only noise was the noise of waves crashing on the rocks in a dead sea.

In that silence, dusk was embracing the night.

Valerio, the young journalist fond of The Dire Straits, got old. He probably still listens to *Money for Nothing*, but surely he does not hear the chirping of seagulls anymore because, in the future depicted in this passage, seagulls are gone. The same goes for journalists, replaced by artificial intelligence, powered by algorithms, and working thanks to fast and immense big data streams.

In this future, preferably dystopic (above all, if you are a seagull or a journalist), we face two issues of the highest importance. On the one hand, ocean pollution that – according to our story – led to an apocalyptic fish extinction and consequently the disappearance of their predators from the shores (actually seagulls are an opportunist species[25], they would have simply changed their habits, moving to a more suitable place: the sunset on the coast, would have been quiet all the same, though). On the other hand, the disappearance of journalists, at least of the journalists we are used to: maybe not so good at adapting as seagulls.

Choices and directions

The first case, with seagulls, depicts the consequence (one of the possible results) of an ominous development trend followed by our society. Environmental pollution is evil, no doubt. No doubt, people need to contain this phenomenon to reduce its impact. On the seriousness of the matter,

[25] Opportunist species, are adapted to exploit available resources even in unpredictable, transient and variable environments. They tend to reproduce rapidly and in great numbers.

there are different opinions. There can be different positions on the possible solutions, maybe according to the various beliefs about the causes. But no one in their right minds would ever think that pollution is a good thing and that environmental safeguard is useless.
Thus, the fight against pollution is not a "choice." Choosing means having different alternatives, making a decision, and face the consequences. Now, the different alternatives and choices in the fight against pollution are related to the possible ways to handle the matter or its priority in the political agenda. There is no other option to preserve our ecosystem. It is a compulsory direction; it can be considered high-priority or subordinated to other issues. But from a merely ontological point of view, it has no alternatives.

The case is different for jobs and professions. The fact that people work better than machines is not so given for granted, nor is it true the contrary. But above all, the two activities must not be seen as an alternative, or even in opposition to one another: Man versus Machine.

From our childhoods, scientific fiction instilled this setting of contrast between human and artificial in our minds. Public debates contributed to consolidate this belief, making it not only believable but almost guaranteed. Actually, it is just of the possible outcomes and not even the most likely to happen.

The different alternatives will come as a result of the melting-pot of conditions and variables partially independent, but also as a result of the choice factor.

Once again, the difference is between "how" and "what":

- With pollution, even according to the different levels of awareness and attention for the subject, the direction is clear; we just need to understand "how" to take it.
- Valerio's case is used as an example to explain the process involving all the jobs, professionals, and society. The point is not only "how," but "what" we are going to do: as people, as a society, as civilization.

Let's go back to the initial question. What kind of vision for the future are we going to embrace? And what will our choices be to embrace that vision, considering that in this complex system, its development is connected not only to our choices but also to an elaborated mechanism of interactions between factors not so easy to control?

(In)dependent variables and conscious choices

Future is the result of a series of choices – partly linked to one another, partly entirely independent for one another – developing side by side with factors utterly free from our will and practically impossible to control (the very same technological progress, in the strict sense, cannot be determined ex-ante). It is clear, then, the difficulty of acting on some of these factors, and it is apparent, for that reason, the necessity to act with strong determination on those factors we can control.

In other words, if it is not possible to control all the possible variables in play, it is fundamental to try and manage the one we can control. Technology, however, is the perfect example to show how such a thing is complicated. And digital transformation is of no help.

Harold Innis[26], a sociologist, was one of the first who tried to disentangled technology, economy, and progress, connected in a non-better-specified relation of cause/effect. He developed his reflections, starting from the concept that technology is at the base of the economic systems. His reasoning begins with an example, to all appearances insignificant: without paper, the modern economy wouldn't have developed. In fact, the paper is used for banknotes and the press, studied by one of his most celebrated disciples: Marshall McLuhan[27]. But the example could be endless. According to Innis, technologies are the engine at the base of social development. That is the birth of technological determinism, with its loyal sup-

[26] Harold Adams Innis (1894-1952) was a Canadian sociologist and expert in economic history, a pioneer in Communication sociology studies.
[27] Herbert Marshall McLuhan (1911-1980) was a Canadian sociologist, philosopher, literary critic and professor.

porters (like Marshall McLuhan) and fierce opponents. In those years, Innis founded his Toronto School, and Charlie Chaplin, embodying the spirit of that period, let people be devoured by the cruel mechanisms of Modern Times[28], in a scene that still today describes the anxiety provoked by the "robotization" of society.

Even if almost a century passed by, and many technologies came in succession, the contrast between social and technological determinism is still alive: there are still many (too many) people thinking that machines will save us, and people preconizing that machines will determine our extinction.
We are the victims of these two opposite behaviors: apocalyptic and integrated[29]. This condition may not be expressed in its form, but it clearly shows its essence in public arguments and politics.
The crucial problem today is that we are laying the foundation of a world and a society that risk a techno-deterministic deviation because they lost their cultural, ideological, and philosophical anchorage of the past century (whatever it was if it was present at all). Still, technologies are not the real problem; it is instead our incapability to co-determinate[30] their development.

Before starting to meditate on the direction to take to shape our future, it is necessary to stop and try to understand the factors on which we can intervene consciously, bearing in mind the different technology applications. And we need to understand the elements on which we have not a say.

Thinking that humankind could control technological development is delusional: history teaches it is not possible. But it is wrong either to believe that society is a mere victim of technological development and that it cannot control any variable.

---

[28] Modern Times is an American film written, directed and played by Charlie Chaplin in 1936.

[29] Umberto Eco (1932-2016) was an Italian semiologist, writer, philosopher, translator and scholar, he wrote Apocalittici e integrati: comunicazioni di massa e teorie della cultura di massa (apocaliptycal and integrated: mass communication and mass culture theories, Bompiani, 1964.

[30] A. Murphie, J.Potts, Culture and Technology, Palgrave Macmillan, 2003.

Progress is unstoppable. In fact, according to history, in the face of technological advancement, there are two possible reactions: one is to act like the English Government, which tried to contain the spread of automobiles by issuing the Red Flag Act[31]; the other one is to try and identify all the right conditions to produce positive effects by exploiting the automobile cultural and social revolution, unstoppable no matter the law.

How? By acting on the variables that can influence the development of any technology.

Which variables?

Research, first of all. There is no need for further discussion on the importance of research in the field of technological progress; lots of authors[32] wrote about it. It is necessary to remember the direct connection between investments in research and development and countries' GPD. This connection underlined that investment in research and development bring about GPD growth. More importantly, it emphasized that the impact of research is proportional to the focusing of the investments: in other words, there is a strong connection between the amount invested and the results[33], and moreover, the results are proportional to the ability to channel the investments strategically. Analyzing the allocations for research in different countries, what emerges is not so assumed: with the same budget, the confluence of well-addressed investments on a selected field of study produces better effects than a mere random fund distribution. That is to say, if a Country's research policy should be the allocation of funds to friends and friends of friends (to be more politically correct: if the funding should be given to all the different actors of the academic ecosystem and the basic research), the results will not be as good as if the

---

[31] Cf. Chapter 1.

[32] In Italy a good summary is the: Relazione sulla ricerca e l'innovazione in Italia (report on research and innovation in Italy, National Research Council, June 2018.

[33] P. Aghion, A. F. Alesina, F. Trebbi, *Democracy, technology, and growth*, Working paper, Department of Economics, Harvard University, 2007; B. Jongbloed, H. Vossensteyn, *Access and Expansion Post-Massification: Opportunities and Barriers to Further Growth in Higher Education Participation*, 2016.

allocation should follow precise strategy lines. Now a question arises: does a strategy for research really exist? Are there any guidelines for the research academies to plan activities to achieve the right goals? Do countries have selected the most important fields of research for investment? Progressive countries that managed to do such things now are vanguard on those fields they were so able to control. All the others are "followers." Like on Twitter.
The capacity to identify the right research policies, supporting them through public investments and incentives for companies, also defines a country's ability to build its future. In 2018, France chose to invest one and a half billion Euro for research on Artificial Intelligences – specifying that laws on experimentation will be less restrictive and offering incentives to international researchers – there are few doubts this fact is going to affect the capacity of the Country substantially to determine the directions of artificial intelligence technologies, using them strategically in the major fields of interest. In Italy, the lack of a framework like that of France, England, and Germany, will bring about serious issues, directly proportional to the political class' ignorance on these matters.

Politics are fundamental. Or at least they should be if they knew what we are talking about when dealing with technologies. Good research policy is not enough to support all the digital transformation processes and allow the Country to benefit from the good impacts and reduce the bad ones (there will always be negative feedback). Political action is needed tout court. Back in the XIX Century, when the English Government issued the Red Flag Act, they didn't achieve the expected outcome. They aimed at preserving the coachmen's job and the railway business. Actually, they only managed to prolong the agony of the sector and limit automobile development benefits, increasing the adverse effects. The result: in few years, the coachmen disappeared anyway, but London was not up-to-date with this changing dimension – even if it led to the disappearance of a job – and missed the economic benefit, it would have caused. "And what about the social impact?" Some would say. The question is legitimate, even more, if asked by a coachman, or – today – by our taxi driver Alfio. The social impact of innovation is always the result of a good vision and a consequent political action. Political actions should not hinder technological development; on the contrary, they should support and promote it.

They should also support the people whose job is endangered by this development. In other words, the solution to Alfio's problem is not to try and stop change: that is not possible anyway. The answer is to nurture it, canalizing the profits produced by the transition to support all those people directly or indirectly affected by it. Real social subsidiarity, not to be confused with a sort of welfarism 2.0. Subsidiarity is a fundamental resource for developing a dynamic balance in society – generated by a more and more fast innovation – to safeguard progress and all the parties: especially the humbles. Not necessarily fastness is an advantage when speaking of social impacts. This means investments in continuing education courses, promoting flexibility, supporting generational turnover, but also taking care of the weaker group of workers. Maybe it's nothing new, but today technology can help us approach these solutions pragmatically, promoting work sustainability, with different feasibility in relation to the past times. Developing a policy for innovation means acknowledging the impacts of technologies on the crucial sectors of a Country. It means understanding the opportunities and the critical points, exploiting the first ones, and minimizing the second ones. Public policy has the power to incentivize certain technologies or solutions created by said technologies. Public policy does not have the ability, though, to stop or undo the effects of digital transformation. Thus, the result of restrictive policies is to obstruct the positive impacts of change but not to eliminate the negative ones. Vice versa, reflecting on the effects of change and trying to control the outcomes will produce measurable benefits in terms of GDP, and above all, in terms of people's welfare.

Companies cannot be passive spectators. The problem cannot be solved only by politics. General education is needed, both in the political class and in the business sector. In Italy – according to research rates[34] - this process is slow and difficult. Our Country occupies the last positions in every ranking on innovation. The positions in rankings depend on the parameters, that is true, but if that position is the same for every scale, no matter the parameters, we have a problem. A serious problem. Not only about skills. Skills are the result of a complex process starting with

[34] For example, the aforementioned DESI (Digital Economy and Society Index), National Report, Italy, 2019.

awareness: if I am aware I have to cross a river and my life depends upon it, surely I will learn to swim. The real complication is that sometimes I am too far to consider it a necessity, and I don't feel the need to solve it. The data at our disposal state that a significant section of the business system is in this situation[35]: at best, they look at the menacing river, both with curiosity and diffidence, ignoring its potential. Plunging into the river is a different story. The capacity to envisage future and innovation like opportunities results from many different variables: the capacity of a Country to build efficient innovation models, the capacity to sensitize young generations and create adequate infrastructures. Even concerning these variables, business culture's role is fundamental; any law or any incentive would be worthless without it. Many cultural contexts believe that innovation comes easily and fast. But it is not possible to deal with innovation in a day or a term of office. It takes time, years, to raise a Country's awareness towards innovation. It takes effort, planning, and investments, involving institutions and firms, supporting managers, and educating people. Institutions' role is to create a favorable background; firms' role is to stop making excuses. It goes for big companies as well as for small enterprises. For small and medium-sized businesses, the innovation path is impervious. Talking about excuses, they think the value of tradition is the justification to avoid the necessity of change. "We've always been doing like this," is the mantra used by Anna's father and uncle, and it's just an excuse to avoid the necessity of change. It is important to preserve traditions – on the production of cheese, to follow Anna's case –, but it is important as well to change what gravitates towards tradition (from logistics to marketing and planning), and it is important to understand that traditions are not immutable. "Tradition is a successful innovation," to quote the great Oscar Wilde: companies look at tradition and innovation as opposites, using the value of tradition as an excuse to overlook digital transformation. But that is a mistake they cannot afford to make. They need to understand the direction of the change provoked by digital transformation to cope with it and be prepared to face it. They need not underestimate or suffer the repercussions, and of course, they need to understand the values of a tradition worth preserving.

---

[35] From the report "L'innovazione come leva di crescita: il punto di vista degli imprenditori" ("Innovation as growth lever: entrepeneurs' point of view), Digital Tranformation Institute – Confcommercio, 2018.

Infrastructures are not optional. Does demand generate supply, or does supply generate demand? The question is Hamletic, and it has been the focus of endless debate in every historical period. However, referring to infrastructures, the answer is beyond doubt: throughout the ages, economic history has utterly proved that the presence of infrastructure generates the development of the services connected to them. Thus, institutions and enterprises (together) have to take on the responsibility of investments to offer strategic infrastructures and the development of efficient services. Infrastructures create development. Development cannot be left out of consideration. Especially when the infrastructure development allows access to benefits that generate growth models opening towards a real change of paradigms. That is the case of telecommunications networks. One of Italy's great *gaps* is the lack of wide-band access[36]. This gap is due to a lack of political vision. The empty space left by politics has been filled by economic actors who directed/steered their actions towards their companies' capitalization, neglecting the Country's welfare. The result was to devalue some crucial infrastructure, such as the access network. The objection "there are no infrastructures because there is no demand" is worthless. Building a bridge does not depend on how many people used to ford the river: the bridge's availability generates the possibility for people to cross it. Of course, infrastructure investments imply – once again – a capacity of vision by politics and enterprises. To develop infrastructures means seeing them as an opportunity. And first of all, it means to acknowledge the potential impacts. The choice to allocate investments to a particular infrastructure can quicken or hinder innovation in some countries. Japan is the most striking example. In the 90s' it was a cutting-edge country for mobile phones production. Still, it chose development models disconnected from the global evolution in this sector (hardware and software infrastructures were not aligned with international standards). From its *first-mover* position now, it is chasing the smartphone market, in which it has found a place only from 2010 on.

[36] Italy's shortcomings in the infrastructure system is underlined, amongst other sources, by the Global Competitiveness Report issued by the World Economic Forum. According to this ranking, Italy places itself in 27th position after France, Germany, Great Britain and Spain.

This created a limited and defined ecosystem (embodied by the "Galapagos mobiles," thus called because their features and characteristics differed entirely from the other products) and, as a negative externality, it also generated a severe delay in the spread of the App market and of the whole platform economy (from social network to e-commerce) with inconceivable economic consequences. The brunt fell on the growth and led to a recovery action, necessary to fill the gap, strongly promoted (and financed) by politics and privates.

The user has the final word. Politics, market, enterprises, infrastructure: they are the main actors to determine the direction and the schemes of the digital transformation that lays before us. But we need to bear in mind that the user has the last word. The market can contribute to the definition of the needs and the consuming models, but according to technology's history, people eventually decide the most compelling technologies. The most persuasive technology is not always the most efficient, technically speaking. People indeed don't choose technological solutions on a mere technical ground: but instead, they decide based on a series of factors, from the real utility to the capacity – often unexpected – for a service to meet a customer's need. Or to adjust to a customer's need. That is the case, for example, of SMSs. They were born not as a messaging system for users, but – only – as a technical answer for the set up of a remote connection with the telephones, allowing the telephone operators to send short messages to the customers. Ten years after their appearance, in 1993, it became clear that customers could use SMSs to communicate. Ten years had yet to pass before the SMSs outnumbered the telephone calls, and SMS became the favorite channel of communication for millions of users. Like WhatsApp, the development of instant-messaging systems slackened and then stopped the growth of a service that remodeled mobile communication aspects (and not only).
Many of us still remember when the spread of video recorders opened the way for the home video market in the last century. At that time, the two main rivals, from a technological point of view, were two standards: the Betamax and the VHS. The first had better technical characteristics. But the second took hold. Why? The companies consortium, investing in the spread of the format, realized that they needed to gather people's tastes and preferences. Therefore, they decided to finance the sector producing

the most exciting content: the porn industry. In a few years, despite the Puritans, VHS spread in many houses and all families. On the other hand, the VHS system had been designed for another purpose: audio recording, but the spread of the Walkman (with lesser-quality devices) undermined the development of the standard in that sector. In this case, the end of the product was determined by a mere ergonomic reason and not by the device's quality: it was uncomfortable to go jogging with a device as big as a video recorder.
We could go on forever, but the essence is the same: the success of a technology is determined by a *mix* of different factors and, from the customer's perspective, the quality of the technology is not always the priority element. The priority element is the ability of that particular technology to grab a need and contribute to the development of behaviors and social habits, which influences the way customers choose their needs. And eventually, how technologies evolve in their direction. A sort of technological Darwinism, according to which the strongest technology is not best. The best is the one able to adapt to survive.

The customer indeed determines the success of a technology, but it is also true that he does not behave like a monad: he lives in a settled social, economic, and cultural context that contributes to the development of his opinions and, consequently, of his consuming choices, or talking about media, of his fruition choices. That is to say that the social actors' ability influences the user's last word concerning technology – the institutions first of all, but also enterprises (for good or for bad) – to determine the cultural and consuming models. The cultural *digital divide*[37] results from the lack of institutions in building a rightful media and technology culture. This culture – like civic education – should be a widespread heritage for society; in this era, it should be a resource, considered as social heritage.

[37] By cultural digital divide we mean the lack of the basic skills to understand the system of the digital media. In comparision to "technological digital divide" referring to the lack of access infrastructure.

Who writes the future?

The future is not written. The different directions of technology depend on society's development, and even if the ways of scientific research cannot be predicted beforehand, it is also true that the direction of these ways is the result of political, cultural, and social choices. Therefore, technological development cannot be curbed, but society can express the addresses to determine the direction. Innovation is not detached from its context; on the other hand, it influences its development, and it is affected by it, in a game of mirrors. So it is true that we cannot choose the directions of progress beforehand, but it is also true that the *input* given by politics and society will always be crucial for its development.

It does not make sense to look at politics and society from a mere national perspective. In this case, technology played a crucial role in the destruction of boundaries, characterizing them as a limit and not as an opportunity.

In this sense, Italy is paradigmatic. Our Country is characterized by two coexisting factors, apparently in contrast with one another.

Italians have always been great users of mobile telephony systems. When mobile phones became smartphones and were used to connect to the internet, they brought about a dragging effect, opening these service platforms to millions of users quickly. The market of smartphones and the related services had such a significant impact we talk about a real platform economy (the main actors in this context are platforms such as Google, Amazon, Facebook, Apple, and Netflix), it is, of course, a global market. The moment a new smartphone is launched on the market, it is available in a few days worldwide. And the same goes for all the services related to the overmentioned platforms. The platform economy's dimension is the lack of any territorial boundaries of the single country. The result is that the customers – in their consuming habits – tend to behave following global styles and standards. That is utterly clear observing the medial consuming behaviors of the young generations. For them, the national dimension is of less importance than trends, styles, and behaviors without any national barrier.

On the other hand, if the users' behaviors – for better or for worse – tend to a process of global technological alignment, it is not the same for infrastructure availability, customers' usage culture, the level of services

provided locally (think about e-government[38] on local ground, or about the digital services of the medium-sized firms: from the marketing to e-commerce and logistics). Regarding these three points, Italy is inadequate: telecommunications infrastructure – especially landlines, which are the backbone of every national network – is underdeveloped with a ten-year-gap compared to the surrounding countries. Customers' usage culture is stationary because while in the rest of Europe, information science and computational logic are subjects taught starting from primary school, in Italy, the government thinks that the issue of the cultural digital divide will be solved simply with the arrival of the born-digital. They were, actually, born when digital devices were widespread. Still, they haven't been taught digital awareness; they run the risk of being passive users, rather than people able to read the complexity of such services and use them to their advantage. The third element – concerning the level of implementation of the services – emerges from the combination of the other two: a lack of infrastructure and a usage culture limited to the fruition of services without a real cultural reflection on their role (at every level: school, university, politics). They produce great difficulty in implementing efficient services to measure up with what people are used to when they connect to global platforms.
A disastrous combination: on one side, the users get used to a level of service which is global and settled by platform economy; on the other side, they live in a local context shaped without any of the crucial infrastructure and culture that should be necessary. They run the risk of experiencing all the negative effects of change without really seeing the possibilities in the change itself.

That is the reason why we need both national strategies allowing the citizens, the institutions, and the enterprises to get the positive aspects of the digital transformation and minimize the negative aspects. We need international alliances to control the ongoing change. These alliances are fundamental to deal with poverty, world hunger, pollution, and define the legislation, the rules, and the etic schemes to influence the evolutional

[38] The e-government is the totality of systems and services of the Pubblic Administration based on platforms and digital processes. These instruments allow the implementation of new services and the enhancement of the old ones, both for the final users or for the other local or national Public Administrations.

process of the platform economy's global actors, having a central role in the building of our future.

Going back to Valerio's story, the dystopic future he lives in describes, on the one hand, the failure of the policies for the fight against pollution, on the other, the failure of the choices regarding the role of technologies in society, specifically of artificial intelligence applied to the information industry.

Once again, we need to remark the difference between a choice and a direction. Fighting pollution is not a choice; it is a direction we must take: the choice is how to do it. The element connected to the disappearance or the evolution of specific jobs is a choice. Political, economic, and social choice.

In both cases, the issue is global: whether we deal with choices to make or direction to take, the effectiveness of a single Country's action is partial compared to global problems.

The environment has no national boundaries; the same goes for the platform economy's multinational corporations, which, today, are laying the foundation of our tomorrow.

This is the moment to define the lines of actions, encouraging the development of a society moving toward the future with awareness and responsibility and not enduring the wrong direction results because of unaware choices. Whether we are dealing with the safeguard of our environment or with the characteristics of the society we want to live in, we are facing global choices: these choices will be decisive to write our future and to determine if Valerio's story will appear as realistic or completely dystopic.

The future between the past and the present

Anna remembered too well those first years when she took the reins of the family business. It had been a hard time. She remembered too well all the sleepness nights, with her stomach upsidedown, doubts gnawing at her, twisting her guts. She was hung in the balance between a past that was not sustainable and a future that looked uncertain. Torn between the promises and the threats of technology, charming in its prospects, but also appalling if considering the risk of not catching up

Mozzarella is just mozzarella; she kept telling herself. There's nothing you can do. Her mozzarellas were the best because she followed tradition. That tradition was passed on to her by her grandfather. She still remembered her grandfather, big, cracked hands and soft because of milk, rennet, and whey. A tired but peaceful look on his face showed awareness. He knew how things were done because they had always been done like that.

But if Anna kept doing things the same way, her company would have come to an end. The numbers were clear. It had been hard to decide what was worth changing, what was worth keeping, what to preserve, and what to revolutionize. Explaining this to her relatives had been the most challenging part. Not to mention the difficulties with her eldest employees! Their skeptical looks, the challenging words, said in her absence, rage, used to conceal fear. It took a long time, a lot of goodwill, faked smiles and hidden tears. A long time before they acknowledged it was for everyone's sake, no one understood at the beginning. This change did not undermine the essence of tradition, the care for the product, the research of quality. The way things were done over the last decades was changing—way before she was born. But computers were not there, at that time, the Net's possibilities, the wonders of robotics that made things more manageable and less stressful, with due respect to tradition. Finally, even the most skeptical employees experienced the advantages of this new way of working! Lesser stress, more time to spend with their families, the possibility to try new things without losing the pleasure, the taste, and the smell of the old ones.

She still remembered her satisfaction, on that day, some years ago: the smell of Spring, with its blooming fields, reached the office. The lawyer looked at her, bewildered. He couldn't believe she was refusing his client's offering, a nameless client, a holding company. Taking the offer would have meant living a quiet life and no need to work anymore. But it would have been a contradiction. All of her efforts to make the work easier for her and her employees, not only more comfortable but even enjoyable, sustainable in terms of time and ways, in one word: pleasant. And she had put a lot of effort into it, and now she had managed to reach her goal; it was crazy to let it go.

From dystopia to dystopia. Anna's future is way better than Valerio's. Valerio's fate is sad, gloomy, and dark; Anna's future is full of hope. Same technologies, same instruments, same possibilities: different futures. And different visions of the future. The fulfillment of one future or the other will depend on the choices of these years.

Individual choices as well as collective, social, economic, and political choices. They will be the result of shared reflections, in which we will find a role for technology, a direction for the development, and a good sense for things. They are choices generated by history that remind us of the intertwined connection between technology and the economy for society's development.

It is useful to look at our past and understand how to look to the future...

Industrial revolutions are not merely industrial

Humankind's history has always been strongly connected to technology. It is no coincidence that whenever we want to refer to a time of significant change caused by introducing new technology in society, we talk about the Industrial Revolution. We talk about it concerning concepts like "machine" and "automation." By the expression Industrial Revolution, we mean those fundamental and irreversible changes that took place when technology produced innovation applied to the way machines work and become independent from men. This autonomy can arise from a new energy source, as it happened with the first industrial revolution; or from the integration of the possibilities offered by an energy source with the production's processes as it happened with the second industrial revolution; from the ability to automize the information processes and information itself, as in the third industrial revolution; from the interaction between the digital logic and the physic world as in the fourth industrial revolution.

The strain/tension of progress has always found its realization in the machines' acquisition of autonomy towards men.

The **first industrial revolution** coincides with the birth of the steam machine by James Watt. It happened in 1769 when the Scottish engineer patented this new technology able to transform pressure, produced by the conversion of water into steam, into motive force. The applications were direct and broad: from transportation to agriculture, every sector became involved, and the concept of industrial production was born. The rise of factories decreased drastically door-to-door jobs: the previous salesmen now had to work in the production facilities. Therefore, the new production techniques permitted to cope with the population's growth thanks to the better yield per hectare of the fields, enhancing food conditions. The engine had freed the men from fatigue, making all the wearying handmade activities more bearable. But things also got another way: far from releasing men from exhaustion, the engine enslaved them somehow. A lot of improvements were made (from medicine to food, and also the reduction of child mortality rates), but in the meantime, a lot of deep inequalities in society arose as well. The new industrial middle class's wealth was provided by the likewise new working class, forced to work inhumane shifts (up to 14 hours in a row) and basically reduced to slavery. It is no coincidence if, just a decade after the steam machine's invention, the workman Ned Ludd destroyed a loom as a protest, starting the movement called Luddism. This movement sprung from the entire working class's appalling conditions and was strangely fueled by the inversion of the cause/effect principle. The effects are still visible today because the technology sector is considered the main cause for the working class's conditions, rather than the use we made in the society of this new factor. That is to say: the question of whether technology is good or evil arose from the first industrial revolution, but still today, we do not understand that it is not merely good or evil; it depends on how it is expressed and applied to the social context.

During the first industrial revolution, a new perception of the industry develops – embodied at that time by the concept of "factory" – and lasted for a long time: that model based on the optimization of the profit, even if to the detriment of the workmen or today – after long struggles led by trade unions – to the detriment of the environment, essential but with no trade union to defend it.

In the first industrial revolution, we find the first hints of a social development scheme, improvable at least, in **the second industrial revolution,** such hints became real consolidated tendencies. The first revolution is mechanical; the second concerns electricity, chemistry, petrol, and the new energy sources. In the second half of the Nineteenth Century, we experience unprecedented technological development. The post-illuminist era, nourished by the Kantian beliefs and the French *ideologues*, sees in technology and technological determinism the key to the development and fastness a condition of convenience. The spaces – thanks to the new means of transportation – compress. Time reduces. The event horizon broadens. Health enhances, underlining the direct connection between industrial development and people's growth.

However, all the conditions above did not always mean an enhancement of the working class's living conditions. The second industrial revolution is the time of Taylorism and scientific management. No doubt, they made a generous contribution to the progress, but they are not an excellent example of sustainability, especially from the working class's point of view. Frederich Talyor focused his speculation on this appropriate assertion: if the production fluctuations are reduced and productiveness becomes constant, efficiency will grow. Practically speaking, this principle, described elegantly by definition "one best way" – based on the approach in which there is just one right way to carry out a process, optimizing the quantity and the quality of a worker's movements – states in a less elegant way the principle of the "ox worker." According to this principle, the workman does not need to ask questions about what he is doing – which is simple and always the same – all he has to do is doing it better. " the research activity and the planning activity are the concern of a specific office; workmen's job consists in the execution of established tasks, broken down scientifically into simple operations, carried out with standard tools and in a fixed period of time[39]."

It is hard to disagree with Karl Marx when he says that the annoying uniformity of an endless job, provoked by a never-changing mechanical work, resembles Sisyphus's torture. In this sense, the very same easiness of the job becomes torture: machine does not deprive men of his job, but deprives the job of all attractiveness[40]. But it is not possible to deny, either, that this Sisyphus' torture is way better than the former situation.

Reality is complex and multidimensional; any other interpretation denying this complexity in the name of extreme simplification should be wrong from the start.

We needed Henry Ford to restore dignity to the workman's job. He used the economic lever to improve his social condition and to increase his living quality.

In substance, Henry Ford made workmen's living conditions better and set an example for other enlightened businessmen, such as Adriano Olivetti. But above all, he proved that the creation of particular social situations does not depend on technology usage, but how it is contextualized in a business plan or a specific chain of value.

Actually, Taylor's production lines are the same as Ford's. However, Ford describes a different model of distribution of the produced values, this model does not penalize the workman, but it encourages him, making him a potential consumer of the products he has contributed to craft. This may seem an outdated consideration, lost in history, but it is modern if we think about some aberrations of the platform economy that often considers the user like a cow to milk, but instead of producing milk, he makes data. These data will be useful to milk even more value out of the user and even more data. This generates an endless loop, that instead of finding its

[39] F.W.Taylor, Principles of Scientific Management, Etas Kompass, 1967.
[40] K. Marx, Capital, 1867

conclusion in the creation of value "for the user," it finds its end when the "value of the user" is consumed.

Going back to our brief excursus on the industrial revolutions that followed one another in the last three centuries, analyzed from the perspective of machines gaining independence from men, it is worth to report Robert Kurz's summary of his introduction to the **third industrial revolution:** "the first industrial revolution is characterized by the substitution of physical human strength with that of machines, while the second is characterized by the rationalization or, for want of a better word, robotization of manpower applied to the machine system. The main mark left by the third industrial revolution was the ability to make manpower unnecessary to the work process and the "rationalization by reduction" of the same workforce thanks to automatic control systems and information systems." The passage is significant because it expresses a fundamental truth (it is unquestionable that because of technologies, the workforce is less central), but above all, it inserts a warped element that influenced all the critics of technology in the last few years. The rationalization by reduction Kurz talks about should lead – in its ultimate dimension – literally to the disappearance of work, but it is far from being applied, not in the third and nor in the fourth industrial revolution. But above all, it asserts that the problem of technological development is that automation does not tend to reduce fatigue, making work more bearable, but it changes the process making the worker useless. This distortion was born with Luddism and spread, slithering through the ages, and finally generating a real techno-phobia up to our days. In the process of object/subject substitution, technology is seen not as an instrument to be developed to enhance our society – as if it were able to create regardless of men – but as something that makes it useless.

The third industrial revolution has guided us towards society the way it is today. This is the society of mass industrialization and the terziarization of advanced economies, of intellectual work supremacy, compared to manual work, of relentless growth – both social and GPD's growth – of immaterial economic activities. In this era, Taylorism is replaced by Toyotism. It is based on the model "just in time." The workman is not just a stupid appendix of the machine, but he becomes a part of the complex process based on the concept of production islands; he confronts continuously with technicians and experts to develop an approach oriented to "total quality."

This is the era of the new world's superpowers. The new industrial and emerging countries aiming to reach economic development equal to that of the first and second worlds. They should be explained. It's not easy to get to that level – in the name of a ripe awareness on the main subjects such as sustainability and environment – with the due limits and restrictions that we didn't consider the issue of respecting. This remains a major issue: we ask those countries, now emerging from poverty, to pay close attention to the environment, to workers, to social rights. But how many of us had, in their development process, the obligations we are asking them to respect? This does not mean that the commitments are wrong. It means that those who did not have to respect them should give practical help to those who are told to respect them. In terms of economics, know-how, and technical support. On the matter, The United Nations have been fighting for a long time now, but at present, the results are not what expected. The impression is that this noble and legitimate request to build development lines compatible with narrower limits to safeguard the world's future – without any adequate support – is just a less noble and maybe illegitimate attempt to keep a power position. Once again, this is solid proof of how complex reality is. It needs to be looked at from different perspectives to try and understand the dynamics.

For sure, today, we can rely on skills, knowledge, and technologies that were missing during the economic boom. That would mean being able to make the difference should these elements became part and parcel of the new economies' development and growth strategies. Technology is the greatest ally of sustainability, even if this alliance is underestimated by those who should acknowledge it.

The third industrial revolution, in the end, it's the era in which the leadership of electronics is passed on to information science; it molds with the telecommunication world and gives birth to telematics. It is the internet's era, and also the age of great possibilities and prospects opened up by the Net. In terms of impact on the economic models, on society, on fundamental rights, on every issue concerning humankind and its living context. But it is also the era of the new ideas related to the freedom of the Web's information, and their confutation made by the same children of the Web. It is an era of great conflicts. The new social and economic context obliges a profound reflection on the growth and development models that ruled the world for over a century.

The fourth industrial revolution

If in the third industrial revolution, information science becomes a critical factor in the economy, with the fourth, the digital role becomes predominant.
Technological development is such to determine a real inversion of power relationships between the digital dimension and the analogic dimension of phenomena. In this world, still so culturally analogic, the digital becomes so pervasive to lay the foundation of the digital transformation that can be defined as a real sense revolution in terms of social, cultural, and economic phenomena.

The race of machines towards independence from the human being is the key we are using to retrace the salient stages of the industrial revolutions that marked the economy in the last quarter of the millennium; it will probably be remembered as the moment when, plagiarizing Neil Gershenfeld, things start to think[41].

Keeping at a distance for now and for an extended period from all the Asimovian's fantasies and goals, with the fourth industrial revolution, in the IoT's era – the internet of thing's age – the digital comes out of the computers and enters inside the objects. By doing this, it modifies the logic, the purpose, and the relations with the customers. Items create information increasingly. In the big data and artificial intelligence era, this information of the users, from the users and about the users is for real the new petrol[42].
The process of change that triggered the development of the digital transformation and that is the starting point of our path starts to outline itself.

---

[41] N. Gershenfeld, When Things start to think, Garzanti, 2000

[42] A. Ross, The Industries of the Future, Feltrinelli, 2016.

As underlined by Klaus Schwab, the fourth industrial revolution is way beyond the concept of "factory 4.0" – with the collaboration of the media simplification – a very popular idea in this period. But what is the relationship between industry 4.0 and the fourth industrial revolution? And again, how is the latter connected to the concept of digital transformation?

The concept of industry 4.0 was born in 2011 in Germany[43]to describe the changing of the global value chain, at the root of the central role gained by the digital in the industrial production process. Big data, IoT, and artificial intelligence give birth to the concept of "smart factory," which goes beyond the traditional idea of a factory and lays the foundation for a context in which the physical manufactural structures are perfectly integrated with the platforms, and digital technologies. They develop an approach in which we have industrial production systems at our disposal. These systems integrate physical and digital dimensions, allowing flexible management of the production equipment.

The idea of industry 4.0 in its origin is strictly connected to industrial production, in which technology is an instrument to maximize the flexibility of production; the concept of the fourth industrial revolution is on a larger scale. It shows the complexity of the digital impacts on society and the economy.

The concept of digital transformation expresses, instead, the social phenomenon that – at the bottom of the fourth industrial revolution – produces an in-depth process of change in the way people relate to technology. To go back to our parallelism, widely used in these pages if industry 4.0 deals with "how" the production processes work, the fourth industrial revolution depicts the shift from "how" to produce and "what" is sensible to produce. This shift is possible, thanks to the digital transformation.

---

[43] The origin of this term is bestowed to Wolf-Dieter Lukas and Wolfgang Walsher, who used it for the first time in a communication, held at Hannover Festival in 2011, in which they announced the Zukunftsprojekt Industrie 4.0, a project of industrial rearrangement to support German economic development.

To summarize: the fourth industrial revolution is the phenomenon that, on the one hand, gives birth to the concept of industry 4.0 and, on the other hand, produces the process of digital transformation involving people and society as a whole. It is the very sense revolution that is redefining; today, the meaning of everything around us.

The moment in which we ask ourselves "what" should be sensible to produce, we underline a dimension of the fourth industrial revolution that goes far beyond industry 4.0: the fourth industrial revolution, in the context of digital transformation, develops a profound change of the balances and the power connections, creating new global actors that are and will be crucial to shape the society of tomorrow.

From Wall Street to Silicon Valley... and back

Today, all those who turned gray will still remember how at the beginning, the Net was considered a possible alternative to finance capitalism that had stabilized a position of power by all means intact. That was the time when in Silicon Valley's garages, all the newborn factories were making history, using the least appropriate definition ever, of the so-called New Economy[44]. This economy should have been based on new paradigms, but inevitably, even if with different dynamics, it was subject to the laws of the market.

In the illusion of a changing world, at the dawn of the New Economy, many – amongst technicians, experts, investors, and financial analysts – convinced themselves that a bigger soccer field, more players running faster, and a new offside rule could be enough to change the game completely. But changing the dynamics and the schemes of a match does not redefine its meaning. Not necessarily. To change the meaning of a game, we need something more: a new interpretation of its aesthetics[45]. These

[44] S. Epifani, Business Community, handling Intellectual Capital in the Net Economy, Franco Angeli, 2003.

[45] In MDA: A formal Approach to Game Design and Game Research, essay published by Robin Hunike, Marc LeBlanc and Robert Zubek in 2004. It explains how every game is made of three elements: Mechanics (the rules), Dynamics (the actions that arise from the application of the rules), Aesthetics (the sense of the game) changing the rules can affect how we play, but not what the game stands for, which depends on its aesthetics.

aesthetics underwent a real change after the birth of this presumed New Economy. They started to change when the digital transformation's pervasiveness developed a social transformation process, of which technologies were the catalyzing element.

The myth of the new economy that produced the vast speculative bubble ever was born in 1994, with Netscape's quotation in the stock market. It was the flagship industry of one of the first browsers to surf on the internet. A series of quotations followed, and the results were so rallying that the usual vicious circle, at the base of every bubble in economic's history was set into motion:

- Investors' complete trust in a product's or a factory's potential;
- Rapid product's price rise;
- An event that sways the expectations of high incomes;
- Great sales fluxes;
- Final product's price collapse[46]

The new economy immediately showed that it answered the old finance rules, but the companies it left as a legacy to the world – despite the fluctuations in the stock market – expressed the potential to change the world. However, the world that was coming out of the crisis of dot.com to enter the more serious crisis of the subprime mortgages started in the first years of the new Millenium and lasted over the following ten years.

When the myth of Silicon Valley started to stabilize on the successes of the first dot.com, it was not only because of the financial interest gravitating around these businesses but also and above all because they seemed to be a real alternative to financial capitalism, portraying the *status quo* embodied by the negative image of Wall Street. To say it in other words, during those first years, Silicon Valley seemed to be definite proof that a counterbalance to industrial and financial capitalism was possible. The union between big companies and finance embodied by Wall Street and Dow Jones seemed vulnerable, in front of the dynamism and Silicon Valley and Nasdaq's fastness. The traditional models, based on slow and

[46] The financial crises throughout history, detailed-study by Consob – national commission for society and stock market, Italian authority for financial markets' surveillance. [source: consob.it]

steady growth, on the need for high assets, on the industrial secret, seemed obsolete compared to the digital approach. These factories were born in garages, they took over fastly, and to the industrial secret, they counterposed new, open models.

But really, did Silicon Valley embody the right alternative to revive the hopes of the American dream? Did it really offer solutions to those problems ascribed to Wall Street's model, solving its flaws and limits?

From financial capitalism to platform capitalism

In the last years, the internet largely contributed to reshaping the world as we know it today. The Net triggered and allowed so great a change that, today, it is hard to remember how the world was before it came. In a thirty-year-period, how people get their information, how they get to know each other, how they choose, how they define their perspectives, how they make friends, how they purchase, how they fall in love has completely changed.
However, it should be wrong and way too simple to look at the social, economic, and cultural revolution developed in the Internet era. It was a monolith set against the old financial capitalism, proposing an alternative scenario.

Looking at the Net's development, we can trace at least four periods, differing from one another on the impacts on society and economy.

The origin. As impressive as it may be, we are not here to recall but briefly the Net's history. We need to start by remembering when the Net – made of few hubs and financed by the American ARPA[47] and NSA[48] - between

[47] Advanced Research Project Agency was founded in 1958, one year after the launch of the Soviet spaceprobe Sputnik, with the purpose to develop American technological skills and oppose that of their enemies. Today the military organitazion is known as Defense Advanced Research Projects Agency (DARPA).

[48] The National Security Agency (NSA) is a governative agency of the United States that, togher with the CIA and FBI deals with national security issues.

the '70s was born from Arpanet[49]. It is different from the actual Net, its systems today are mostly outdated, but the concepts of distribution and de-centralization are already its strongholds. The impacts on the economy are still limited. The internet is just a research project, and not so many people can read its potential.

The dawning, the nerd period. When the internet left the research facilities and the universities and took its first steps in the world, the reality was full of researchers, technicians, engineers, and experts. This system developed around this wider and wider net of enthusiastic people from all over the world, with different professions and different experiences. It is a real Golden Age for the internet. At this stage, we are getting to know the people who are preparing to shape our society. They are pioneers in a new world. These people define a new common language, they develop characteristic behaviors, they write the social rules in a newborn context, they tie inseparable alliances, and at the same time, they create deep hostilities and cultural and ideological contrasts. The concepts that are going to define the destiny of the Net are taking shape during these years. It is the net of the sharing, opening, free software, information as a right, hackers. It is a Net that – still today – raises a nostalgic smile for those who remember it. That is the Net crowded with nerds. It is the evolution of the concept of a nerd. This concept helps to understand the deepness of a change in conceiving the relationships between the internet and society. The origin of the term "nerd" is uncertain[50]. Still, the concept is clear: it is someone who tries to get over their difficulty to interact with

[49] It was designed for military purposes during the Cold War. The Advanced Research Projects Agency NETwork (ARPANET) was a net of computers designed and realized in 1969 by DARPA. From its embryonic form, in 1983, the internet was born.

[50] There are three possible origins for the term "nerd":

1. It appeared for the first time in 1954 in the book If I Ran The Zoo, by Dr Seuss. The text says: "A nerkle, a nerd, and a seersucker too!" the term then is used as a name for one the animal in the book;
2. It is the acronym of Northern Electric Research and Development, a company in which all the employees used a pocket protector, a protection against ink dots. The acronym nerd was printed on this pocket protector;
3. It derived from the word "drunk", read back to front is "knurd" and was used to refer to people who did not consume alcohol at parties. [source: NerdGazmo]

other people by devoting themselves to the technologies. They sometimes use the technologies as an instrument to mediate interpersonal relationships. In the beginning, the definition of Nerd had a disparaging connotation. We read in Google Dictionary: "an unstylish, unattractive, or socially inept person, *especially* one slavishly devoted to intellectual or academic pursuits and devoted to the new technologies." Bill Gates[51] is a nerd. Linus Torwalds[52] is a nerd. Even Steve Jobs[53]is a nerd.
Nerds are the creators of the first great internet age, laying the foundation for the years to come. In the decade between the end of the '70s and the '80s, the popular imagination depicts the Net's image, considered as an alternative to multinationals' excessive power. The Net is seen as a participatory democracy regulated by a set of non-written rules. These rules are based on meritocracy and open-mindedness and focused on the principle that a sustainable alternative to Wall Street's financial capitalism is possible, thanks to the communication technologies. This climate brings about the phenomenon that with its Killer application[54] gives birth to the Net.

The development, the geeks' civilization. On the 6th of August 1991, Tim Berners Lee, an unknown researcher in Geneve's CERN, published the first web site. If we want to find a divide between the nerds' era and the next stage of web development, that is undoubtedly the best. The web is the instrument through which the internet could reach the general public made of privates, companies, and institutions. These are the bases for its diffusion, becoming more and more exponential. The development of the web coincides with that of PCs and then with that of the mobile network. The Internet's era is based on the merging of the media into the digital. It triggers, starting from the communication devices, a digitization process of entire business branches and society itself. First, computers and then mobile phones (changed into smartphones technologically redetermined

---

[51] Bill Gates, full name William Henry Gate III, is an American business man, programmer, computer scientist, and philantrop. He was the founder of Microsoft Corporation.

[52] Linus Benedict Torwalds is the Finnish programmer who invented the first version of Linux, the most common open source Operating System in the world.

[53] Steve Jobs (1955-2011) full name Steven Paul Jobs, was an American businessman, computer scientist, and inventor. He was the co-founder of Apple.

[54] The concept of killer application describes the application or the service thanks to which a new technology is widespread and penetrates the market.

by a pervasive Net) produce a radical change in people's behaviors. The Net's impacts are disruptive in the most different sectors. Every company, every institution, every individual has to deal with a society-in-changing. Once again, semantics helps us to understand the impact of the event better than digits and numbers: those nerds, considered by society as outcasts, ha planted the seed that was remodeling that very same society from its roots. Technologies are not instruments for misfits, and they are not used as a substitute for personal communication. Nerds start to be creators of relationships. The young people now using technology are not considered outcasts by their peers; they are models to emulate. If Steve Jobs was a nerd, then his iPhone – and iPod[55] before it – are a cult. The change is so sudden that we need a new term to identify people who use technology; the negative term "nerd" is no longer suitable. The term geek[56] is dug out. If the nerd was considered as an outcast, the geek is regarded as an upright person, an example. It is hard to consider the billionaire Mark Zuckenberg[57] as a misfit nerd. Slowly, the term nerd loses all its disparaging meaning, and it is used to describe a person who uses technologies and deeply knows them. The fact is, all those people that back in the '80s were considered as the nerds' community had the great merit to depict what we now in the 21stCentury call geek's society—a tremendous existential payback. But the geeks' civilization somehow betrayed the principles that caused its birth.

The present, the platform era. With the geeks' society, we arrive at present times. The Net was the protagonist of a change path that produced the results we are experiencing now. The Net spread rapidly and developed even more quickly. It became something completely different compared to what it used to be in the beginning. In time, the nerds who iden-

---

[55] iPod is a digital music player launched on the global market by Apple on the 23rdof October 2001. A music player with a reduced size, its technology based on a hard disk and a flash memory.

[56] The term geek in the beginning is used with its negative meaning of "crazy", "fool", and "weirdo". In XIX Century's English it was used to describe freak characters in circuses and festivals. Today it lost its negative connotation and it applies to the subcultures next to the information science's and digital technologies' world.

[57] Mark Elliot Zuckenberg is an American computer scientist, and businessman, known to be one of the five founders of Facebook.

tified themselves with the ideas of sharing, open-mindedness, and cooperation contributed to delineate a Web utterly different from what we had in mind. In the collective imagination, the web was seen as a sustainable alternative to financial capitalism's aberrations. Actually, it used the same levers of finance – magnifying them thanks to the digital possibilities – to set the stage for new capitalism. Nick Srnicek[58] defines it as platform capitalism. The platform capitalism results from an age in which "The Big Five[59]" and their epigones are shaping models for the production of value. They are based on the rising ability to extract data from the users, to create higher incomes, but without giving them back a proportional value. In substance, the Net should be open, as much as the companies – born on the web and thriving on the web – are based on closed business models. The web should be based on a model of shared management of the value, as much as the capacity to create value is based on the centralization of the information extracted from the users. The Web should use cooperation to create shared value, as much as the great platforms are based on their ability to intercept that value and organize it according to proprietary models. The Web had envisioned the disintermediation possibilities as much as it created new and more powerful intermediaries. The Net was set on the free access of information, as much as the prevailing business models are based on the development of *walled gardens*[60]. People who enter feel at ease, but their walls are high, and once in, it isn't easy to exit. Platform capitalism contrasts with financial capitalism. This contrast is not based on the proposal of a model inspired by the principles of sustainability. These principles should guide defining the rules of a change path, oriented towards a better economic system. Platform capitalism uses against financial capitalism the effects of the very same aberrations the Net wanted to fight in the first place: closure towards collaboration, power centralization, the ability to extract the value without giving it back to the context where it was taken. The

[58] N. Srnicek, Platform Capitalism, Polity Books, Cambridge, 2016.

[59] Apple, Amazon, Google, Facebook and Microsoft.

[60] With the expression walled garden we refer to a closed platform or a closed digital ecosystem. A service that restricts the fruition of authorized products and makes it hard for the customer to reach contents and applications using different sources from the platform itself. The best example is Facebook, that forces the users to make use of contents, news, videos or applications through the platform itself instead of using freely the World Wide Web.

side effects of digitalization amplify the situation. On the one hand, digitalization allowed people to get their information freely and widely, enhancing society. On the other hand, it gave power to those who control the information. In this case, platform capitalism, far from reducing the aberrations of financial capitalism, will increase them. The familiar feeling about the "good" Silicon Valley, seen as the alternative to the "bad" Wall Street, has rapidly changed Americans' point of view. The same Donald Trump decided to use it speciously as a crucial element of his political campaign for the presidential elections.

We write the future (as well)

Today, we are at the dawning of the platforms' age. This age still needs to define itself in its characteristics and its shape. The face of society, in the next years, will depend on this profile.

The platforms can be an asset for the economy and society, or, in the shape of a self-creating entity, they can devour everything around them and not give back to the ecosystem the value they are taking from it. This will depend on the choices the world is going to make in the years to come.

The right to information, privacy, the concept of freedom itself are the themes at stake. The freedom to acknowledge, choose willingly, preserve the private sphere, be in contact with the world, and be aware of how this contact is redefined through cognitive and interpretive filters. The platforms will be able or not to raise those filters, being the intermediaries between what we experience and what is hidden.

Today in our world, we need to be indexed on a search engine to be visible; not being present means to disappear before the interlocutors' eyes. The outlooks of a highly connected society, depending on this connection, are related to the algorithms' management. They will define the boundaries between known and unknown, acceptable and unacceptable, accessible and inaccessible, present and absent. The algorithms, powered by big data, will lead the artificial intelligence, complex and crucial for everyone's life. The big data will be governed by the rules we have the responsibility to write.

If we want to understand what kind of future lies ahead of us, whether it will be Valerio's future with his seagulls or Anna's future with her mozzarella cheese, we need to reflect on the rules.

The rules that will determine the algorithms but first of all, the rules that will define our society.

The rules we chose until now led to a blameworthy economic growth model, but they also produced general welfare. The level of awareness we reached gives us the chance to reflect upon our next steps and our following choices. It would not have been the same as other models. History teaches. But today, we are facing a turning point: we have the responsibility to define our next steps both on individual and collective grounds. We have to decide what to keep and what to change about the model we have been using until now. This prospect can trace a path with the possibility of a comparison between different social and economic approaches. Some things worked until now, but it does not necessarily mean that they will continue to work without the necessary corrective actions. We need to keep that in mind. No doubt, Capitalism brought about significant advantages to western civilization. But what can we do today to make the whole world thrive harmoniously?

Anna, the businesswoman. And Valerio, the journalist. Anna's and Valerio's are two parallel universes: they are determined by the choices we will make regarding society, economy, and environment. The role of technologies will be crucial. Digital transformation, acting as a catalyst of change, could be either the maker of a positive development or a stop to welfare.

The future that lies ahead will depend on how we interpret the digital transformation as an instrument of social, economic, and environmental sustainability.

We were better off when things were worse. Or maybe not

Alfio's shift had just finished. Eight hours in a cab were not a cure-all. Besides, one cannot choose the clients. He needed a good beer with the right friends to forget it all. After all, he had no time to complain about his job and didn't want either: he had to make plans for next week-end to the seaside. He was almost fifty, two marriages behind his back, but he never stopped being such a prankster.

Life is long; he kept telling himself. And full of opportunities.

Alfio works. He goes out with his friends. He makes plans with those friends. He is in his fifties, he has been married twice and has still a lot to do. Alfio the taxidriver, how he is described here, is the paradigm of ordinary. This normality is made of good things and bad things, obstacles to overcome, and opportunities to take. This is the everyday life for millions of Italians, for millions of Europeans, for billions of western citizens. It is not normal for Indians, for the Chinese, for the third and fourth World citizens, they would not consider Alfio's situation as normal. What Alfio sees as normal is the achievement of modernity, the result of a development model that proved – apparently – to be valid, more than others. This development model gave the western world a high welfare level. What is normal for us is entirely utopian in other contexts or the prerogative of privileged groups of people: from the average life duration to the possibilities of life, from the connection between work and spare time to the very living dimension of the concept of opportunity.

It's not taken for granted that what has been working until now will continue to work tomorrow.

Technology did us right

Alfio's story becomes irrealistic not only if we steer from the western world to other areas but also if we stay in Europe but turn back time. We don't need to go too back, compared to the long man's history, if we want to change the game.

Let's take as an example a symbolic moment: 1861, the declaration of Italy's Unity. If Alfio were a coachman, instead of a roman taxidriver of the second millennium, even his age would have been extraordinary. In 1861 the average life's expectations were 35 years, rising to 49, not counting the high number of children dying before 5[61]. Today a fifty-year-old man is in the prime of his life: 150 years ago, he would have been decrepit.
Alfio has three children. Back to Count Cavour's time, to grow three sound children, you had to make at least five, considering the death rate. After work, Alfio has time and strength to have a beer with his friends and plan a weekend to the seaside. In 1861, the reality was different: the working class, after a 12 up to 16 hours shift, had not so much energy left to spend at the weekend. They had no weekend anyway because the working week was made of six or even seven days. On Sundays, one did not have the strength to read the newspaper, but that was not a big deal because about 75% of people were illiterate.
Italians were a population of economic migrants: between 1861 and 1913, over 20 million Italians sought their fortune abroad, leaving their homes in wretched conditions, and facing difficult journeys. In most cases, with no hope of coming back home. (it is impressive how Italians seem to forget their past in the face of what is happening today).
At any rate, short memory or not, Alfio is living peacefully; he still has infinite opportunities in his fifties. Had he been born less than two centuries ago, he would have lived a very different existence. Hardly better.

"We were better off when things were worse." State the nostalgics of the past time, but they did not actually live during that time. Times of sicknesses, wearying work, missing human rights, and a huge social gap.

[61] V. Tanzi, the economic and social conditions in Italy around 1861, Rubettino Editore, 2013.

What changed from that time? In this transformed society, the scenario is entirely different. Technology had a crucial role in this change.

By retracing the history of the industrial revolutions, one acknowledged how the technological aspect has always been a fundamental human development element. It helped to enhance the welfare level, even if its dynamic is complex and controversial. Scientific and technological research improved people's health conditions and also introduced all those changes that produced tangible and concrete benefits for life. Not only about the lifespan but also about the quality. The growth of life's expectations, the better access to culture, the lessening of physical strain, the reduction of the working hours in favor of spare time, the possibility to travel, the opportunity to learn and know, to evolve and grow. These options are the result of technological evolution and its impacts on society.

These impacts – it must be said – were not entirely positive. The difference between Taylor and Ford is narrow, but it is not technology's fault. It depends on the growth model that – with technology's help – we choose to follow.

Don't shoot the pianist

Choosing a social and economic growth model means embracing its values and flaws, trying to focus on the first, and trying to minimize the second. However, men incline to acknowledge only the positive aspects of the chosen model, pretending the negative ones do not exist. Trying to ignore the flaws of the selected model comes not without consequences. They will eventually become not so easy to ignore.

The problem is – considering that in the complex maze, which is the society, we are like pilots who cannot control the steering wheel – that when the flaws become so big that it is not possible to ignore them anymore, they are also too severe to solve them. Anyhow, we find ourselves in this situation.

The concept of capitalism identifies a social and economic layout developed in Europe at the dawn of the feudal system, back in the Middle Ages.

It established itself globally as industrial capitalism during the following centuries, thanks to technological development and high capital confluence. In its basic definition, capitalism is based on fundamental elements such as the ownership of the means of production and the distinction between them and the producers, creating a free labor market; the possibility to hoard money. "In capitalism, the market, generally speaking, acts as a coordination system to allocate and distribute the goods. Thus, capitalism and the market economy are strictly connected to one another[62]."

One of the main side effects, according to Marx, is the tendency to gather assets to create profit rather than to satisfy the needs of those who produced them. It is the distinction between capital and work. According to Marx, it is the contrast between the orientation to create wealth (by the capitalist) and its use to enhance the conditions of those who produced it (the worker).

Critics of capitalism are not new. They started with capitalism itself. Ages and technologies followed one another, philosophers and economists followed one another: the context changed, technology changed, the world changed, but the subjects are more or less the same. As a result, when we discuss today the impacts of technologies such as robotics or artificial intelligence on work and the workers, we face the same arguments that Ned Ludd faced when he (allegedly) destroyed the famous loom.

The critics of capitalism are serial and repetitive. Rachel Jaeggi, professor of practical philosophy at the University of Berlin, classified them into three different categories, wholly detached from the period and the context: they are functionals, morals, and ethics[63].
The firsts state that capitalism cannot work as it is: that is to say, according to the functional critics, capitalism is naturally dis-functional and subject to a crisis. There is no way.
The seconds – that Jaeggi defines "morals" – state that capitalism, whether it works or not, is immoral because it is based on exploitation. According to this critic line, "it denies people, unjustly and unfairly, to

[62] R. Jaeggi Immanent Critique of Capitalism as a form of life, Rosenberg & Sellier, 2016.
[63] R. Jaeggi Immanent Critique of Capitalism as a form of life, Rosenberg & Sellier, 2016.

enjoy the fruits of their labor, it puts people in slavery, in a system that deprives them of what should be due[64]." According to this line of thought, capitalism is based on an unfair social structure, and it also creates new ones. It keeps getting better and better.
Last but not least, Jaeggi identifies the critics revolving around the ethic sphere: "a life molded by capitalism is terrible (alienated, for example). Life is depleted, meaningless, void. The essential components to living a human and satisfying life, a free life, are wiped out. To be brief, capitalism leads to alienation and is based on alienation[65]."

According to the three categories of this analysis, everything revolves around the concept of "exploitation." According to the critics, this concept is irremediably and indissolubly linked to capitalism itself, with a negative meaning. If we consider these two concepts as inseparable, it is hard to think about capitalism as an ethic, let alone moral, mostly if the idea of exploitation is seen as naturally negative.

However, we need to consider what we said at the beginning referring to Alfio's lifestyle: capitalism, compared to all the other economic models, engendered positive outcomes.

John Macey and Rajendra Sisodia[66] underline:

- Two hundred years ago, 85% of the population lived in extreme poverty. Today it dropped to 16%;
- The global income pro capita raised by 1000%, from 1800. It increased by 1600% in developed countries.
- Americans' living quality standard raised 10000 times from 1800;
- In the last 200 years, average life's expectations raised from 29 years to 68. They become 80 in developed countries.
- In the last 40 years, the undernourished people's rate dropped from 26% to 13%;
- In less than 200 years from total illiteracy, we descended to 16% for adults;

---

[64] ibidem
[65] ibidem
[66] J.Macey R.Sisodia, Conscious Capitalism: liberating the Heroic Spirit of Business Harvard Business Review Press, 2014.

- Economic welfare growth led to the growth of democracy and freedom: 53% of people live in regular Government, elected by universal suffrage. One hundred fifty years ago, the rate was, simply, 0.
- Data show how the life satisfaction index is closely related to the country's economic welfare: the life satisfaction index, for people living in the quartile of the most developed countries, is 7.5 out of 10, while for people living in the last quartile is 4,7 out of 10. We were better off when we were worse off. That is not so true, after all!

So, it is too easy to shot the pianist. We point at the warps of capitalism, but it is challenging to find a valid alternative or at least an alternative that could produce the same widespread welfare.

The world did not manage to find one, up to now.

Can exploitation be sustainable?

Jaeggi underlines that the problem is about the concept of "exploitation" connected to capitalism.
Because if we consider the values of exploitation to be intrinsically harmful, our critics have no way out. But if the concept of "exploitation" had a different significance, things would change. Between the idea of children's exploitation and the idea of soil exploitation to grow vegetables, the difference is enormous. The first case is beyond any reason. In the second case, we need to ask ourselves what limits we need to fix to make exploitation possible.

If we abandon the radical assumption that no exploitation is possible because all exploitations are evil – like vegans with their honeybees – then our argument takes another turn.

If we flank the word "exploitation" and the word "sustainable," we open a new ethic dimension of capitalism that goes beyond the protestant Weberian's setting and aims to what some call "ethic capitalism." This capitalism believes that the welfare of society in its entirety is essential to obtain a long-term profit. The leading multinationals started to promote this vision. This definition has been used in a vision statement of the Business Round Table, an association of the foremost American companies' CEOs. They also stand for the development of public policies oriented to improve the citizens' welfare.

Greenwashing[67]? It may be. Even if it is a façade operation, it says something about the prevailing feeling of the companies. They are realizing – firmly – how those themes draw the attention of the citizens. It doesn't matter whether the alleged turn of the ethic capitalism is a real tendency of the big industries or just a marketing expedient.
This turn is the symptom of people and society's growing attention towards this issue. Whether it is a right turn or not, the change process is set in motion.
That's what happened in the first half of 2019 with Greta Thunberg[68]'s "case." The critics towards the Swedish activist divided the world into two factions: the fans and the haters. According to the fans, she had the merit to prick the young people's consciences, urging those subjects that should be the big companies' prerogative. According to the haters, and that is the most shared option, she was a mere instrument of the multinationals (themselves) to steer the attention from other "issues." The "bad" multinationals were under the spotlight, no matter the perspective. Few reporters underlined the central point: regardless of the young activist's opinions, Greta Thunberg's "case" showed us that an environmental conscience exists amongst the young generations. The themes she talked about, intentional or not, are taking interest and attention. The young generations will look for a future based on new models, different from the actual ones—the same young people who will decide the future.

---

[67] The term greenwashing was used for the first time in the second half of the Eighties by the American ecologist Jey Westerveld. It refers to the communication strategies and projects used to build a deceptive positive image about environmental safeguard to deflect the real activities and the damage the create on the environment.

[68] Greta Thunberg is a Swedish, environment activist, known to be the leader of the movement "Friday for Future". At the age of 15, between August and September 2019 she started to "strike for climate", refusing to go to school to go on the street and protest against the politicians and their indifference for climate issues. The echo was immense and she became a symbol for millions of young people all around the world.

The devil you know...

Out of this perspective, it would be a mere rearguard battle to keep reasoning about capitalism being good or bad, net of any academic argument. Asking if capitalism was good or bad until now loses its importance, compared to the necessity of understanding how it needs to change to interpret a transformed society's needs.

The first reason is that, obviously, if a model has been the better solution for that period, it doesn't mean it will be applicable in the future. A good model is declined inside a specific economic and social context, and forgetting this assumption is as wrong as stating that this model is always the worst.
It is wrong to look at the world from a techno-determinist perspective, and it is wrong to think that only economic models can redefine society's meaning. A capitalistic society is nor good, not bad by itself. But capitalism can be good or bad depending on the social choices – individually and collectively – made by capitalists. These choices depend on the cultural context, on the awareness, on the social inclusion of particular behaviors: a vast totality of factors not utterly dependent on the economic dimension. They will help define it.

The second reason is more complex and less noticeable. The change processes are not linear. But human beings tend to treat them as if they were linear. We think that a complex system – no matter which: a country (think about GPD), a company (think about the revenues), or a calf (think about the weight) – needs to grow following a regular constant to develop correctly. Hans Roesling calls it the "straight line instinct[69]."

In the actual world, things don't work like this.

When a baby is born, he's about 20 inches long. Over a year, he grows about 11 inches, 31 in total. If the calculations are correct, it is about 60%. If that percentage growth were a constant, our child would be 16 feet tall

[69] H. Roesling Factfulness Ten Reason We're Wrong about The World and Why Things are Better than you Think.

in five years. Not to mention the room that his parents should rent for his sweet sixteen's party!

Clearly, something is wrong.

A five-year-old boy is about 3 feet tall, on average. The trend is more or less constant until puberty when in a few months, the height increases by several inches. As if boys had been plunged in fertilizer. In the development of a human being, every period has a specific growth rate. An altered rate is always pathological, and the outcomes are always wicked. The same goes for a calf's weight or any other living being, and the same also goes for other complex systems. Factories, with their assets, countries with their GPDs. In other words, thinking that the economy should grow at a regular and steady rate is like thinking that - in Biology - living organisms should continuously grow from their birth to their death. Looking at economic growth as a crucial development factor was not wrong. On the other hand, data prove that it increased the welfare lever on a global scale. However, that same goal, which basically produced advantages over the last decades, could stop providing benefits and start creating a lot of damage if settled in a different period of development of our society.

A child cannot score a 60% growth rate per year all life long, and the same goes for the economy. It cannot increase several percentage points every year in a country's history. It is suitable for a child to take 11 inches during the first year of life. But it would be catastrophic should he take the same inches in the following years. The growth of the skeleton system would damage the other systems, causing the body to collapse.

The same goes for the economy. If the economic growth rate were constant for more than the necessary time for that growth to produce positive impacts, the economic system's growth would damage the other elements of our ecosystem: the environmental system, and the social system, for instance.

The time has come. An economic system based uniquely on the GPD's growth runs the risk of becoming one of the worst autopoietic[70] systems. They grow, feeding on the energy of adjoining systems, but they give anything back: parasites.

Many people underlined the limit of GPD. The very same Simon Kuznets who created it. He tried hard to explain that GPD wasn't a wealth index and referred to it as "the most used and misunderstood index in history.[71]" Robert Kennedy's opinion on the matter is famous: "We cannot measure the national spirit on the basis of the Dow-Jones, nor can we measure the achievements of our country on the basis of the gross domestic product (GDP). Our gross national product counts air pollution and cigarette advertising, and ambulances to clear our highways of carnage. It counts Whitman's rifle and Speck's knife, and the television programs which glorify violence in order to sell toys to our children. It counts napalm and the cost of a nuclear warhead, and armored cars for police who fight riots in our streets. Yet the gross national product does not allow for the health of our children, the quality of their education, or the joy of their play. It does not include the beauty of our poetry or the strength of our marriages; the intelligence of our public debate or the integrity of our public officials. It measures neither our wit nor our courage; neither our wisdom nor our learning; neither our compassion nor our devotion to our country; it measures everything, in short, except that which makes life worthwhile[72]."

Bob Kennedy reminds us that the GPD does not measure the welfare; it specifies the sum of every product made by a complex system, for better or for worse. And as a paradox, the total provided by GDP doesn't show society's actual welfare.

Going back to our child's metaphor, it would be the same if we tried to determine the child's health by reading the addition of all the parameters

---

[70] R.H. Maturana F. G. Varela R.Uribe Autopoiesis: the organization of Living Systems, tis characterization and a Model, Biosystems, vol.5 pp187-196 May 1974

[71] E. Masood, The Great Invention: the Story of GDP and the Making and Unmaking of the Modern World, Pegasus Book, 2016.

[72] Robert Kennedy, Lecture at the Kansas University 18th March 1968

in his blood test without knowing - or discerning – what should be high or what should be low.

Complex systems and technology

Like a calf's organism, the society we live in can be described by all means as a complex system, which is a dynamic, multicomponent system made of different interacting subsets. Interacting implies that the actions produced on a single subset can affect the others. Thinking that one of them could grow steadily for an unspecified period without affecting the other subsets would be not only wrong but even dangerous.

It is dangerous for two reasons: the first reason, as we said, is that it would generate an imbalance in the other systems connected to it. The second reason is a consequence of the first: in a complex system, the resilience of an element compared to the others is not limitless. It means that the changes taking place in a system endanger the other, and moreover if we analyze two connected subsets, and we operate a change in one of the two, the other collapses.

In other terms, going back to our child, the rise in body temperature is a defense mechanism caused by pyrogens (for example, a virus or bacteria the child took in kindergarten or at the park): the rise in temperature generates a reaction of the immune defense system with the production of antibodies and other defense cells. Fever is an instrument used by the body to defend itself from an attack. It is a positive reaction if one can control the temperature. If it is too high, the virus will die, but the side effects are not so pleasant. One can even die. Suppose a system develops an action that goes beyond certain limits, the risk is to produce an adverse reaction in another system.

To think about it, it happens the same when the technological system meets the social system.

A couple of examples will do to explain the concept. Computers' computing skills increase exponentially. It raises so fast we already exceeded

the limit supposed by the famous Moore Law[73] (that, by the way, is not a law, in the strict sense).
With the rising of the processors' computational skills, the quantity of information they can process rises. But does the elaboration skill of the human brain grow simultaneously and with the same rhythms? And what happens when people are in an information system that produces exponentially more data than they can elaborate? What are the consequences – social and also neurological – of the prolonged exposition to all these stirrings? And – even assuming that the increase in information is not a problem itself because the same technologies used to produce it can also be used to filter it – what happens in front of such a deep change of the information ecosystem, in which the human being is not in contact with information, but with meta-information filtered by algorithms? And what happens if, during the meta-information's evolution path, the human being cannot comprehend it anymore?
Generally speaking, when the analogic universe meets the digital universe, they engender an imbalance due to the two worlds' different resilience. Whether the first is based on physical limits and on a material dimension that is characteristic of its being and typical of the human, the second is so flexible and fast-changing that it is simply impossible to apply in a physical context.

At the dawning of quantum information science[74], human limits are an element to take into consideration. We need to be aware that the possible evolution is not always sustainable. In our world, the speed of change is growing progressively, but we have to keep in mind that human beings' capacity to assimilate it cannot go at the same pace.

---

[73] The first Moore's Law, more than a law it is an empirical observation. He postulated that the number of transistors that can be packed into a given unit of space will double about every 18 months. The complexity of a microcircuit, calculated for example by the number of transistors per chip will double every 18 montsh (and quadruple every 3 years). Gordon Moore, toghether with Robert Noyse, is the founder of Intel, one of the most important producer of microprocessor in the world.

[74] The quantum information science uses the laws of quantum mechanics and quantum physics to elaborate data. Instead of the digital "bit", taking the two values 0 and 1 it uses the qbit that can be simultaneously in both conditions. It can be defined as the sum and the study of computing techniques, using quanta to memorize and elaborate information. This allows computers to be faster and high-performing and to redefine, together with information science all the connected fields.

In the path of progress, we are now in a moment of landmark change. It is the phase in which our child stops growing several inches per month and his growth pace changes. The trend changes because the previous rhythm wasn't suitable anymore, and his body needs something different.

Technologies and capitalism. Two elements of a complex system that need to be put together with the utmost attention. Technology – as a catalyst – has the power to speed the growth trend in a way that should be fatal to our child. But the very same technology also offers the possibility to build the right conditions so that the world, having new instruments, achieves a general wealth level. It will use new growth models enabled by economic paradigms based on the digital.

These paradigms are inspired by the awareness that the complex system we live in, our ecosystem, is the result of precarious balances that can be easily broken. The concept of sustainability must be the central focus of the individual and collective choices; it must be considered the pivot around which the world's future revolves. Sustainability reminds us that every choice we make in the economic, social, or environmental fields has consequences. Sustainability reminds us that, in every complex system, each change in one of the components generates feedback on the others.

Capitalism allowed our taxidriver, Alfio, to live a comfortable life, better than if he were born a couple of centuries ago. It enabled him and many of us to obtain wealth – the contents being equal – that wouldn't have been possible with other models. However, according to capitalism and a mutated social and technological context, our modern society is endangering Alfio's job. It forces us to reflect on the direction we have to take starting from tomorrow. We need a high awareness to take this new path, in the light of the latest and powerful instrument at our disposal. And digital technology can be the best ally, crucial for the building of a sustainable world.

Sustainability as a cultural model

It was the crack of dawn. The twilight was turning to daybreak, speckling the sky with a reddish tinge. The cool night breeze was making way to the heath of a June day. Swallows had started to come and go, flying in their nests, under the barn's beams. Domenico was already at the greenhouse. Like every morning. The silence of dawn, no customers, no workers, it was the perfect time to lose himself in his reflections. He was looking with a critical eye at his seedlings, thriving in the plateaus. He attested to their well-being; he judged the quality of the seeds. Sometimes he was content with his decisions; sometimes, he complained about things he could have done better. The plants would be ready for sale soon enough, and all his fatigues would be rewarded. Trimming some overgrown buds, he thought about his work and how it had changed over the past years. He was thinking about the importance of choices. His decision to be one of the first in organic food production made him the leading nursery in the area. Organic food: who would have thought it possible some years ago? The certification seemed to be a whim, but it was becoming a significant share of his revenue. He was smiling at the idea of this strange situation. He spent years considering chemicals as a conquest, and now he was changing his course. He still remembered his grandfather's rage for the infestation of parasites. They ate all the plants and destroyed months and months of hard work. He remembered his father's satisfaction when he started to use the first pesticides. Now his father was a retired but still active man and looked at him both with a bewildered and amused expression on his face. He used to look at him in that way every time he told him that those useful pesticides couldn't be used anymore. That look made him lose his temper because he was right: those pesticides were beneficial. If he used them now and "pumped" his plants with a bit of fertilizer, not of the kind on the procedural guideline, he would have dropped the loss and optimized the profit. No one would have noticed. Not with the frequency of the inspections. Indeed his income would have been higher and more effortless. But at what cost? A price he didn't want to pay. He told himself while he was crushing a bug, crouched on a tomato.

The price Domenico doesn't want to pay is not only the price of his honesty but also the cost of sustainability.

It was the price of having a smaller quantity of plants and slower growth cycles because he didn't want to pump them with fertilizers full of hormones.

If Domenico decided to play dirty and bypassed the procedural guidelines using non-permitted substances, he would probably have an economic advantage. Presumably, it would also be a significant advantage. Some of his colleagues don't care about not respecting the rules, and they don't fear being discovered by the control organisms, knowing their difficulties in the inspecting procedures.
It is not for fear of a sanction that people like Domenico choose to respect the guidelines. It is for the awareness that the price of sustainability is actually an investment.

It is an investment because, in a social context that cares about the environmental safeguard, the clients appreciate the value of those who have responsible behaviors. They prefer with resolution all those operators that can be reliable and attentive towards both the environment and their clients. And that, of course, is good for the incomes. But Domenico's choice is not only economical. It is based on the awareness that producing healthy products will safeguard his collaborators. And the environment he lives in. And that will be his children's legacy.

In short, Domenico's choice is sustainable.

What is sustainability?

Domenico's reasoning is not complicated. It is quite understandable, linear, and straightforward. And it is founded on a just as much straightforward concept: sustainability. It is no coincidence that the United Nations, over 30 years ago for the first time, referred to it as: "meeting the needs of the present without compromising the ability of future generations to meet their own needs."

Then it goes on: "Yet in the end, sustainable development is not a fixed state of harmony, but rather a process of change in which the exploitation of resources, the direction of investments, the orientation of technological development, and institutional change are made consistent with future as well as present needs. We do not pretend that the process is easy or straightforward. Painful choices have to be made. Thus, in the final analysis, sustainable development must rest on political will[75]."

This definition takes its inspiration from the theory above of systems. In substance, society – as a complex system – needs to act, bearing in mind the crucial goal: improving humans' living conditions. It needs to operate without unbalancing the other complex systems: people, economy, and environment.

Going back to the child's growth – or the calf's weight – it means that the current rate of two inches per month or a kilo per day in the calf's case is good for the first year of life (both the baby's and the calf's), but past that period the same percentage related to the overall height is not sustainable. Trying to keep that pace is just an illusion that can compromise the system's complex balance, whose levers are only partially activated by human intervention. It is like driving a car and controlling one of the four wheels: it is possible to steer, but the bending trajectory is uncertain. We risk hitting the wall.

The world lived its first year: in which a child grows two inches a day and a calf one kilo a day. It was the age of the three industrial revolutions, the era in which capitalism led us towards what we are now, the era in which we laid the foundation for the so-called fourth industrial revolution.

Now we need a different growth rate, not to unbalance the system. Taking the best out of modernity, we need development models to build a sustainable path.

When we talk about system balance and about unbalancing it, we think immediately about the environment. It's there for all to see how human

[75] Our Common Future, World Commission on Environment and Development. Overview of the United Nations, 1987. Also known as Butland report.

actions modified the ecosystem: it is not a negative thing itself, but it happened – and happens regardless of the other species and the future generations – that we broke that intergenerational pact proposed by the World Commission on Environment and Development in 1987.

Sometimes we don't think – and the results can be devastating – that when we speak about sustainability, it is not enough to think about the environment. Still, we need to put into action other variables corresponding to just as many other "systems:" economy and society. Without these variables, any reasoning on the subject is pointless. The reason should be obvious: altering one of the three variables produces impacts on the others. These impacts are usually directly proportional to the variation's entity. But often, they risk becoming exponential.

A simple example connected to biology. If human stature doubled, the consequences on the skeletal system wouldn't be linear: the thickness and the density should triple and not double to sustain the weight of the body because the surface of the bone section grows on a quadratic scale while the volume of the body, the weight, grows on a cubic scale. Even a small change in one of the system's subsets risks producing modifications to such an extent in other systems connected to it. The problem (amongst others) is that the relations between our complex system's subsets, in this case, environment, economy, and society are many, are intertwined and difficult to identify. Thus it is not so easy to understand what reaction corresponds to the action.

Environmental, economic, and social sustainability

Environment, society, and economy are not merely connected; they are the parts of a whole. To make his life easier, our nurseryman Domenico could use a pesticide made of neonicotinoids[76], illegal according to the procedural guidelines. That would cause a decrease in parasite-produced pathologies, enhancing production and consequentially of the income.

---

[76] These pesticides based on neonicotinoids act on certain kinds of receptors in the nerve synapse, blocking the transmission. They are much more toxic to invertebrates and honeybees.

But there are two risks, at least. First, the area would be thoroughly polluted in the long run, with potential problems for himself and his colleagues. They would be at risk of diseases, and that would lead to costs for health treatment. Second, the idea of breaking the rules would be risky – on a juridical ground and, of course, on a reputational ground – in case the fraud was revealed.

Suppose the reverse situation: Domenico, to improve the general condition of resource exploitation, plans to reduce the density of crops or eliminate any attempt to contrast the damaging insects.

This action, even if thought to safeguard the environment, would affect the company's profitability. The activity – under the production parameter – would be unsustainable from an economic point of view. This would lead to a financial breakdown, and it would mean a social breakdown for a family-run business.

The economic, social, and environmental systems are always strictly connected: whatever action is made on one of the systems, there will be impacts on the others.

The starting point: environmental sustainability. The word sustainability initially is thought to be intrinsically connected to the environment dimension (the concepts of economic and social sustainability are introduced officially in the second half of the Nineties[77]). The assumption is that the Earth's resources cannot be exploited indefinitely. The connections to this principle are not merely ethical and moral, also physical: the first law of thermodynamics reminds us that energy can be neither created nor destroyed, only transformed. The second states that every time energy transforms, we have energy expenditure and an increase in entropy. Regardless of (scientific or not) trends and beliefs, the climate crisis results are that in the long term, the world will face severe issues without serious environmental sustainability models[78].

[77]The concepts of Economic sustainability and Social sustainability are officialised in in 1995 by the United Nations' World Summit for social Development.

[78] Environmental sustainability means to guarantee the availability and the quality of the natural resources ensuring the fulfilment of the needs of the present generation

There is no management of the environment without impacts on the economy: economic sustainability. The sustainable management of the environment implies responsible management of the resources. On the one hand, it makes things complicated; on the other hand, more interesting. This fact connects the subject of environmental responsibility to that of the economy. That is why we talk about economic sustainability. There is no possibility to manage local or global policies without determining substantial impacts on the economy. Whether we have to run Domenico's nursery or Anna's livestock, or on a bigger scale, a country's economy, our choices to safeguard the environment will come to terms with economic sustainability. What we said before about capitalism refers to this point: economic development engenders retroactions on the environment, and they need to be tamed if we do not want to doom the future generations' destiny. Economic sustainability[79] assumes an economic model respectful of this principle.

If we speak about the economy, we end up speaking about society: social sustainability. It is clear that the economic model infers – and generates – the social model of reference. The technologies at the base of Taylor's models are the same used by Ford, but the results, as discussed, are quite different. Thus, it is not possible to talk about economic sustainability without referring to social responsibility.

And here, the "noble" dimension of sustainability (what kind of society do we want?) and the "manly" dimension (what are we inclined to give up?) come into play.

Of course, it is easy to depict theoretically the kind of society we rather have: without hunger, wars, poverty, pollution, social injustice, and so

---

without compromising the possibilities of the future generations. This concept was born from the study of the ecologic systems and envisages load capacities, automatic control possibilities, resilience and resistance which together affect the stability of the ecosystem itself.

[79] The concept of sustainability starting with ecologic aspects becomes broader, taking the economic dimension into consideration. This definition envisage progress and welfare going beyond the wealth rate and the economic growth based on the GPD. Economic sustainability implies a steady and growing welfare, with the prospect to leave the future generations a better living quality. This implies also public debt sustainability and "industrial setting" sustainability.

forth. But it is difficult to come to terms with the fact that what we "theoretically" want produces impacts on what we "practically" do to obtain it: just as if Domenico were an activist against pollution but did not want to give up using chemical fertilizers to keep his production rate high. Everyone has their vision of society, and often it goes beyond what generates immediate impacts on our lives. These impacts are difficult to digest when they are imposed as conditions for sustainable development. That is to say: we are all sustainable with other people's commitment.
In this sense, social sustainability, meant as the capacity to guarantee the conditions of human welfare (safety, health, education, democracy, participation, justice) equally distributed by class and category, is the most important of the three. The models of society come from it, and the scheme of values and priorities come from the models. Thus, there is no possibility of developing strategies oriented towards economic and environmental sustainability unless based on the ideal of society we want.

First of all, the subject of sustainability is a cultural matter. We need a real culture of sustainability. That is to say; we need to look at the Earth as a complex system made of inter-operating elements that need the definitions of tactics in the short term and strategies in the long term. Absolutisms and apocalyptic points of view are useless. Extreme visions as well. They do not help us to face the subject of sustainability pragmatically. Nonetheless, we need insights and ideals to build sustainable models of development.

Digital sustainability, in this complex model made of relations between the systems, is a support element. It will enrich environmental, social, and economic sustainability representing an enabling element and also a key to the technology. It will orient technological development, as it happens for the environment, economy, and society, towards a precise sense model. In this sense, Enrico Giovannini speaks about the Digi-circular economy[80] underlining the connection between the circular economy and the digital economy. They work as connective elements of the necessary transformations to enable what he calls "sustainable utopia":

[80] E.Giovannini L'utopia sostenibile (the Sustainable Utopia) Laterza, 2018

the energetic, the education system, and the monetary system. digital sustainability becomes an enabling element of "Digi-circularity."

From the Brundtland Report to Agenda 2030

Sustainability's path has been long, but it is enough to start going back to the second half of the Eighties' to understand the actual situation.

In 1987 the Brundtland Report described sustainability as fulfilling the needs of the present generation without compromising future generations' possibilities. In that period, the approach towards the subject of sustainability was intrinsically connected to environmental issues.

Thanks to the Report and the reflections developed during that period, people started to conceive that the environmental dimension was just one – even if the most obvious – of the dimensions to consider to deal with the problem. We had to wait a few more years before the two economic and social sustainability concepts were outlined. It happened thanks to Agenda 21, a document issued in 1992 at the Conference of the United Nations in Rio de Janerio. It is a landmark for the subject. For the first time, 178 Governments subscribed to a document that defined common guidelines to act for the promotion of social, economic, and environmental development to build a sustainable world.

The results were not as hoped. Most countries' commitment turned out to be wavering and connected to local policies rather than to strategic plans aiming at the future of the world. However, the 27 principles[81] of Rio define a joint development model that embodied the fundamental transition in the path of sustainability.
They talk about the environment, of course, but they deal with it in the light of a new dimension. They underline that the ecosystem concept depends either on the economic models, that require new, global, and responsible approachesand on the capacity to control innovation and technology to use them as support to sustainability[82]. They also talk about

[81] Cf Appendix 1: Rio declaration on environment and development
[82] Principle 9

young generations, women, connections between the local and the global spheres when dealing with pollution, models for identifying environmental degradation based on the intersected subsidiarity of countries. At that time, the nations were not able to establish their global policies on the three "Es" (economy, ecology, equity); nonetheless, they could determine some choices that will influence the path of sustainability the way we know it today.

The following step was the issue of the Millenium Development Goals[83] (MDG); the heads of state ratified them at the Millenium Summit of the United Nations in 2000. Agenda 21 marked a change of intents, while MDG was also a preliminary success in the outcomes: extreme poverty halved, according to the goals, the access to education and health facilities enhanced. These are tangible facts.

But the very same promoters, in Oslo Conference of 2015, had to admit that – because of the issues connected to environment and climate – we were far from achieving the goals.

These problems are connected to scarce governance skills and the lack of experienced UN Agencies[84]ready to support the process. We need to bear in mind the complexity of such an operation. For the first time in men's history, the main target is the coordination of humans' attempts to defend and safeguard the models and the principles, utterly unknown up to this point. It takes time to break in the engine. This time was used to work on stabilizing the United Nations' organizational apparatus, creating the conditions to support the processes, and working on identifying the driver to set a framework of global governance focused on sustainable development.

States should cooperate to strengthen endogenous capacity-building for sustainable development by improving scientific understanding through exchanges of scientific and technological knowledge, and by enhancing the development, adaptation, diffusion, and transfer of technologies, including new and innovative technologies.

[83] Cf. Appendix 2: the Millenium Development Goals

[84] The United Nations Agencies are autonomous organizations born to deal with specific issues. Nowadays they deal with different and various questions: labour (ILO), food (FAO), science, culture and education (UNESCO) and Health (WHO).

The most vital driver was – uniting the indissolubly economy and environment – the affirmation of the green economy, an expression that comes from the Summit of Rio 2012, dedicated to Sustainable Development. This concept defines the model according to which it is necessary to deal with the problem globally. The resolutions need to start with the idea that hunger – even in the outermost places – is incompatible with the concept of sustainability itself. The essential elements should be rebuilding a degraded environment, the welfare of the citizens achieved through the enhancement of the living conditions, taking into a count the peculiarities of every population and the different levels of development. This is not just a moral or ethical question but also systemic: it is impossible to solve a problem locally if that same problem is not considered in its complexity.

It is necessary to restart the Millenium Development Goals with a more concrete approach. They need to define global policies considering either high-level goals and more concrete and also specific targets.

It is the birth of Agenda 2030[85]in New York. A three-year work and eight-negotiating-sessions to define the 17 Sustainable Development Goals described in detail in 169 Targets. They aim to develop a global partnership dealing with social, economic, and environmental sustainability, both globally and according to the single country's reality.

The importance of Agenda compared to the previous projects is various: it defines the systemic approach to the subject of sustainability; it defines the model of the general targets in global and local contexts; it defines the measurement system, based on multidimensional and rigorous indexes for the implementation of United Nations' control structure. But above all, it defines the goal around which we need to organize the big countries' development policies, in the awareness that sustainability is not an option, but the only possible way to build a better future.

The 17 goals for sustainable development to achieve within 2030 may not be perfect, may not be reached, maybe modified along the way. But they

[85] Cf. Appendix 3 the sustainable development agenda 2030

stand for a purpose horizon and a temporal horizon. We need to look at these horizons to have a clear, concrete, and shared target.

The target becomes concrete when we ask ourselves about the role of digital technologies in building our future. Considering technologies as instruments to create a better world means considering them as instruments to help us achieve the 17 Goals.

Which sustainability?

In this holistic approach towards sustainability, in which environment, society, and economy are the components of an inseparable whole, it is crucial to have a look at the resources that come into play and the modalities to handle them, on the basis of political and social choices.

Whether Domenico the nurseryman uses or not certain kind of fertilizer, whether Alfio, the taxidriver's competitors have or have not a license and use a private car, whether Anna, the businesswoman, is obliged or not to declare the provenance of her milk, the question is the same: how do we use the resources at our disposal?
Do we instead support the development of a free market, or do we orient ourselves to a green economy model, built on the necessity to decrease our resources' impact? Do we rather preserve our resources, or do we want to exploit them? Are we positive that the free market will ensure (inexplicably) the infinite renewal of the resources used by humankind? Are we positive that a growth decrease is a fundamental step not to endanger future generations?

Choices to be made. Choices that create a model of society and an approach to sustainability. This approach is not dictated by Agenda 2030; it derives from the different strategies the countries will choose to support in order to fulfill the goals of Agenda 2030. They will be determined by a political vision of the society we want to build, balancing between two approaches: techno-centric and eco-centric[86].

---

[86] K.R. Turner Economics of Natural Resources and the Environment

These approaches diverge essentially for the different ways of managing renewable and non-renewable resources at our disposal. They are a real patrimony (economic, but also natural and ecologic) that define society's balance according to the way we use them.

- The **techno-centric** approach is based on the economic factors' preponderance on the environmental factors separating in very weak[87] sustainability and weak sustainability[88]. In the first case, the society should be oriented to the total exploitation of the resources, without restrictions on economic development, believing that nature has a merely instrumental value at humankind's disposal. This is the model followed by the first three industrial revolutions, also because of their ignorance. They thought that our resources were limitless and could be used with no hesitation, regardless of the future generations. Today this model is unsustainable, but it shows a difficulty: it is a suitable option for all those countries that did not experience the three revolutions and that today are facing progress in the same perspective of the western world at the time of the steam engine.
    - In the case of weak sustainability, the tendency to economic growth is predominant, but it is also controlled by more considerable attention towards the management and preservation of natural resources. The supporters of this principle believe that economic growth should be based on the resources preservation principle, according to which the capital must remain steady in time not to compromise the rights of future generations. Nature is an instrument, but the concern for other people and the concept of intergenerational equity surface.
    -

[87] Robert Merton Solow, On the intergenerational allocation of natural resources The Scandinavian Journal of Economics vol. 88, pp. 141-149 March 1986

[88] D. W. Pearce, G.D. Atkinson, Capital theory and the measurement of sustainable development: an indicator of weak sustainability. Elsevier Science B.V. Ecologial Economics vol. 8 p. 103-108, October 1993.

- On the other hand, the **eco-centric** approach is based on the preponderance of the environmental factors over the economic factors profiling strong sustainability and very strong sustainability[89]. Strong sustainability posits a world with a null economic growth, in which the orientation to safeguard the natural resources is connected to the collective interests. They prevail over the private and individual interests, in the view of ecosystem preservation. The strong sustainability posits the safekeeping of the natural capital through actions protecting the non-renewable sources and guaranteeing the renewable sources' reproducibility. Suppose the strong sustainability posits a null economic growth. In that case, the very strong sustainability considers the reduction of economy and population an imperative, with a decrease in consumer goods finalized to reduce the resources' impacts. According to this approach, moral rights are above all others. They derive from merely justice beliefs. Without superior rights, it is impossible to enjoy the others: for example, the right to life is superior to good living quality.

The four different approaches to sustainability differ in one element: the balance on the management of the resources on the basis of their impacts on the social, economic, and environmental systems.

The aberrations of the two antipodes: very strong sustainability and very weak sustainability, are substantial. Today an approach based on very weak sustainability is clearly not acceptable. It is not only in opposition to all the international treaties but also in opposition to common sense. It is also difficult to accept the idea of very strong sustainability, according to which the ecosystem always comes first of any living being dwelling on it. In the first case, the unscrupulous orientation to marketing growth would destroy the environment. In the second case, the feverish attention to the ecosystem would hinder human beings.

[89] R. Costanza, Ecological Economics: The Science and Management of Sustainability, Coulumbia University Press, 1991

Technologies as sustainability catalysts

It is difficult to find a guise, but technology can be an excellent ally. If we deal with sustainability as system logic, our best instruments are technology and digital technology. That is why we need to reason in terms of digital sustainability.

In the first chapter, if we hark back to digital transformation, there are at least two dimensions we need to take into account:

- **Technology as support of processes.** It is what we defined as the "how" dimension. Technology and digital help us in the redefinition of how we make things. The instruments offered by technology allow us to read the events, explain them clearly, and intervene effectively. Technology can help us handle what we do in a better way. Better means in a more sustainable way. The possibility to use the telecommunication network made Valerio's work easier. The opportunity to use precision farming systems enables Domenico to diminish the use of chemicals, thanks to sophisticated sensors detecting his crops' parameters (chemical value, humidity, parasite presence). Indeed technology and digital enable us to improve what we do, optimizing the relation between efficiency/effectiveness. This optimization can be used either to produce profit according to a model that is not sustainable anymore or to contribute to the building of a sustainable world. It is a matter of choice.

- **Technology as a change creator.** It is what we defined as the "what." Digital transformation does not limit itself on the impacts of the processes, but it represents a condition that redefines and redetermines the dynamics of many social schemes (from how we communicate to how we get information, from how we intertwine to our purchase or political preferences) developing a change in society. This change forces a reflection not only on how we make things but also on what it is sensible to do in light of the profound transformation that technology is producing in the world. Digital transformation is not a transformation "of" the digital but a modification on society activated "by" the digital. Also, in this case, if the sum of this change is positive or negative will depend – as we discussed in this chapter – on ourselves. It will depend on our choices, our beliefs, our way of resorting to technologies. It is a landmark change of the "what," and the orientation towards a better and more sustainable world is not so given for granted. Technology puts us at a crossroads. Once again, the choices are not only economical but deeply ethical and based on values. They will be influenced by our way of looking at the future. If society will be based on the value of sustainability depends on us.

In the definition given by the Manifesto for Digital Sustainability,[90] the role of the digital in society passes through two elements: the direction we can give to the development of technologies and the retroaction that technologies produce on people, economy, and environment during the change process. these elements are indissolubly connected and strictly interdependent, and in this context, we do not have to ask whether technology is "good" or "bad." Technology is neither good nor evil, but it does not mean that it cannot create effects in both directions. It is fundamental to ask ourselves about the negative impacts to minimize them. And concentrate on the positive impacts to give them value. From this perspective, we need to understand how technology is functional to humanity and not the other way round. For this purpose, we need to guide the developments to produce positive impacts on society, setting as a real instrument of sustainable development.

Thinking about sustainability without looking at the opportunities given by technology and digital transformation to achieve the goals, we run the risk of transforming the concept of sustainability into a paroxysmal version of degrowth[91]. Or in a romantic and naïve version of the "happy

[90] Appendix 4: The Manifesto For Digital Sustainability by the Digital Transformation Institute

[91] S. Latouche, La scommessa della decrescita (the bet of degrowth), Feltrinelli, 2007.

degrowth,[92]" we run the risk – instead of basing our principles on sustainability – of seeking refuge in crops fertilized with the horn manure.[93] Technology can be a catalyst of sustainable development, enabling the optimization processes (also enabling huge savings, both on a microeconomic and macroeconomic level), and it works like an articulator of the different components that create our system (environmental, social, and economical in the first place) simplifying the creation of models based on information that should be impossible to acquire and make valuable without the help of technology.

Digital transformation can urge the development of cultural and philosophical models inclined towards open-mindedness, sharing, and cooperation. It is not a case that the greatest conquests of technology were born in contexts oriented in this direction. It is not a case that the models of "open" innovation were born in this branch. We need to remember how the concept of sharing that engendered the sharing economy is activated by the digital. The sharing economy itself reminds us that the high-moral-value principles, exemplary as they may be, run the risk of becoming prey for marketing operators, ready to change their social value into revenues.

This fact underlines the importance of developing a strong cultural dimension around the subjects of technologies for sustainability.

Sustainability culture and technology

"Sta mano po' esse fero e po' esse piuma" (my hand can be as hard as steel or as gentle as a feather) Mario Brega used to say threateningly to Carlo Verdone[94]. The same goes for technology. Like we said. Technology can

[92] M. Pallante, La decrescita felice. La qualità della vita non dipende dal PIL, The Happy Degrowth. Living quality does not rest on GPD. Editori riuniti, 2007.

[93] Horn Manure, commonly known as "500", is a technique of biodynamic farming postulated by Rudolf Steiner obtained by the transformation of high-quality cow manure that has been put into cow horns and buried under the earth for the winter period. Once become hummus it is melted in water and dispersed in the fields to structure the soil.

[94] The film "Bianco, rosso e verdone" made in 1981 was produced by Sergio Leone and distributed by Medusa under the direction of Verdone himself. One of the most celebrated scene is that of the roman actor Mario Brega acting as a threatening truck driver.

be a sustainability instrument. Even more, it can be the greatest ally of sustainability. But suppose we want technology to be a concrete instrument for building an efficient and sustainable development model. In that case, it is necessary to develop an unprecedented cultural operation to promote the correct use of this tool.

Our assembly line can be Taylor's alienating one or Ford's sustainable one. The development direction depends on such complicated factors that are not possible to control, but partially it depends on concrete choices—made by society and politics. These choices must be conscious.

Thus, it is fundamental to develop a cultural dimension related to technology. We need to emphasize a sense dimension in which this cultural dimension can pursue the sustainable development goals, fixed globally, whether we refer to Agenda 2030 or to whatever our targets will be.

It is not assumed that technology is an ally of sustainability. It will rest on us. The first step is to develop a real shared culture of technology at every level of society as an instrument of sustainability.

Here comes the importance of introducing the concept of digital sustainability into public arguments.

To do that, we need to acknowledge both the possibilities unfolded by technology and the threats it carries. We need to know its strength and its weaknesses. We need to develop a widespread awareness about the instrumental dimension of technologies and their impacts on a social, economic, political, and environmental level. The first step is to get to know the technologies.

Technicians make them work. What we need is the insight of technologists. They have to read their sense and understand the implications of the economy, society, and environment in a framework of digital sustainability.

03.

The instruments of change: what is what?

The tiles of the mosaic

Anna was seated at the cashier's desk. Despite her busy schedule, she had always wanted to stay in close contact with her clients. She liked human contact. Everyone considered it a waste of time, and she had to tell herself that she was doing it to understand her clients' tastes. That is why she had decided to keep a factory store. She enjoyed peeking at people from behind the screen, looking at how they moved along the aisles, trying to figure out which product they would have chosen.

Back in the days, it was the best way to get to know the customers, to figure out their tastes. Today she could have done without it. She had invested a great deal in technologies, but it was worth it. Every client had their ID, and she was able to acknowledge their tastes, their purchases, and even the batch of the products they had bought.

She remembered too well how hard it was to convince her father to scatter all sorts of gadgets in the factory. Sensors and devices he claimed he did not understand. The truth was, he understood them too well; he was just frightened. Their presence in the factory reminded him that the world was changing. But looking at him now, playing with his tablet with those big hands, made her so proud. He got to like his tablet. He didn't use it to play but also to check the production and the sales in real-time.

To wake her up from her thoughts, Mrs. Elvira's stick, ticking on the floor: eighty years under her belt. And they were all visible. Anna saw Elvira's indecision; she went close to her favorite cheese and then made do with a cheaper one. So Anna took Elvira's favorite cheese and hid it, to give it to her once she had checked out. But with discretion, like when Elvira used to give candies to Anna as a little girl.

An amused smile opened on Anna's face. Thinking about her childhood, but also thinking about Elvira's hesitancy. No artificial intelligence would have noticed. Nor any artificial intelligence would have presented her with a pecorino wheel.

Not until now, at least. She thought with a shudder.

Technologies as an instrument to fulfill the sustainability goals fixed by Agenda 2030. An instrument to make people's lives easier, build a more comfortable setting, enable economic models aiming at the promotion of human welfare rather than mere profit. Technologies to facilitate the change, focusing on the beacon: sustainability.

What kind of technologies are we talking about when we refer to what is called without awareness and with different meanings digitalization, digital transformation, or industry 4.0?

Digital ecosystems

The most common mistake when talking about technology is to think that "one" technology can solve the problem. There are what we call *killer applications*, that's true. They enable a system's breakthrough. Taking the Internet as an example, its killer application was the Web. That is to say – before the Web was born – the Internet was less known, less accessible, and less common. If Tim Berners-Lee had not invented the World Wide Web, maybe the Internet would not have been so widespread; it is not assumed that it would have played this role in society. And more, there would not have been the Web, which is based on a single network protocol[95], if there weren't for a set of factors. These factors consist of other protocols connected to the Web[96]and the spread of suitable web infrastructures such as the spread of PCs and the investments in time and money made by factories, people, and institutions to create the first websites. For PCs, the interfaces based on windows were crucial; for the development of smartphones, the *Apps'*model was essential; bitcoins were essential for the blockchain. And so on.

Every single technology is based on a real "ecosystem" of other technologies that simplify the spread. They are activated one by one, and for

[95] The standard network protocol of the web is the HTTP.

[96] We refer to TCP/IP (transmission Control Protocol/internet protocol), they define the standards on which the internet is based. Without their help the development of the HTTP protocol, at the base of the Web, would not have been possible.

many different factors, they speed up the entire ecosystem's development process. Moreover, the ecosystem is made not only by technologies but by a complex set of elements and players that revolve around them. They enable the spread and make them pivotal for society. We talk about "digital ecosystems," that is to say, "socio-technical systems, open, distributed, adaptive, with self-organizational proprieties, scalability, sustainability inspired by the natural ecosystems[97]. In other words, digital ecosystems are composed of both technological components (such as the Net, computers, smartphones) and extremely social factors (such as people and organizations). They are usually open because, together with coopetition[98], these are the innovation processes' best development instruments. It is not a chance that the concept of openness is often connected to that of innovation, mostly when we talk about digital.
From the *open-source*[99] to the *open standard*[100] to arrive at open innovation models, the topic of openness – of the software source code, the standard, and the business processes – is essential. Openness is considered a generating-innovation element, developing a positive change thanks to contamination, debate, and growth.

[97] G. Briscoe, P. De Wilde, *Digital Ecosystems: Evolving Service-Oriented architectures, BIONETICS 2006*, Proceeding of the 1st international conference on Bio inspired models of network, information and computing system, ACM Press, 2006

[98] It is a business strategy combining the characteristics of competition and cooperation. (P.T. Cherington,1913).

[99] At the beginning, the term open source defined the software with a license used to enter to the source code. The definition after the work of the Open Source Initiative becomes more complicated and well-structured, with the addition of several characteristics (from the possibility of the programmer to speficy that the original code is kept unchanged to the obligation that the trade licence is not discriminatory for people, groups, or sectors of usage). It is different from the concept of free software, born at the beginning of the Eighties.

[100] An open standard refers to a format or a protocol subject to a complete public evaluation, royalty free, and complete availability for all the parties; devoid of every component or extention deriving from format or protocols violating the definition of open standard; free of every legal or technical clause limiting the usage for users or businesses, ran and developed freely by any distributor in an open process with equal participation of competitors; available in different implementations made by competitive providers for all the subject in a non-discriminatory way. (source: European Interoperability Framework – EIF European Commission).

Anyway, these systems develop mutual interdependent dynamics between the elements, making them very similar to the natural ecosystems.

A digital ecosystem is made of several elements and different players that go beyond the single technology. On the other hand, they can determine its waxing or its waning.

The main:

- **Telecommunication companies**. They develop the physical infrastructure to connect to the Net, the essential framework.
- **Private and public research institutions.** They develop the technologies and determine their usage;
- **The education system and universities.** They (should) guarantee the transmission of knowledge and competencies necessary for the development of innovation processes and paths;
- **Tech companies.** They are the technology industry and develop products, systems, and services which are at the base of digital transformation;
- **Platforms.** The giants such as Facebook, Google, Amazon, and Apple that transmit the information and the service, linking the customers and creating value for them and themselves (in questionable proportion);
- **The companies.** They access the set of services present in the Net and (sometimes, hopefully) they take advantage of the opportunities;
- **Trade unions.** In this landmark climate, they can use digital transformation to redefine the sense of their role as support of the industries;
- **The users.** They should be gravitating core, but due to various and not always positive dynamics, they end up gravitating around the whole situation.

Some natural digital ecosystems develop under lucky or specific circumstances, and some others are produced on purpose to support and foster the development of digital and technological innovation. These ecosystems are planned and realized by combining forward-looking public policies favorable to innovation and private investments aimed at profiting from it.

The American Silicon Valley is a historical example, and also what has recently been called "Silicon Wadi," the Israeli Silicon Valley. Either way, we are facing models that aim to develop digital innovation to foster growth models. It is not assumed that this growth should be oriented to the goals of Agenda 2030. After all, It is not assumed that technology is used for constructive purposes either.

Which technology?

If we want to retrace the path of innovation, we need to think in an ecosystem logic.

In Anna's case, it is clear that the young businesswoman didn't use "one technology" to renew and upgrade her company to the rhythm of an ongoing changing world. She resorted to the sensors of the Internet of Things to track the production process of her mozzarella cheese; she developed a platform to access the data provided by the sensors and guarantee the traceability; she put in some public blockchain the traceability information for the utmost safeguard of the customer (or for the marketing). Furthermore, she used the internet connection, widespread all over the factory, to install webcams for her customers to check on the production and health of cows continuously. She uses social media to interact with her customers and the digital platform for online sales to go beyond the local boundaries. She flanks e-commerce with a local retail network; she gives value to the data acquired by her clients by using the *omnichannel* logic. With this logic, the factory can regroup together the clients' data no matter where or how they were generated, handling all the sales channels coordinately. From what she says, we can imagine that she uses an upgraded customer relationship management, able to infer the tastes and preferences of the buyers and trace their behaviors through combined tracking systems of their online activities and in-shop technologies (present in the shop). These technologies are used both to track the client and to enhance his purchase experience: the *customer experience*, so crucial in the *social media* era.

In conclusion: there is not just "one technology" that enabled Anna to face this complex change process but an organic set of intercommunicating solutions. They work together to solve Anna's problem, which is to offer in the best way her mozzarella cheese to a more and more significant group of customers.

It would have made no sense for Anna to choose a single technological solution, following the latest trends or the marketing aggression of the information technology system. It is too often focused on achieving income targets more than solving the problems of the customers. It has been crucial for Anna to set in motion a development path built on the ecosystem logic: she decided to cooperate with a local research center for the identification of the best options, support the continuing education of her operators, assist the local agricultural institution in educating the best students to be hired, dedicate her time to build a partnerships network.

It was not the blockchain, the Internet of things, or the big data to solve Anna's problem. It was her ability to choose the right mix of strategies based on technologies to support her business model.

What are then the tiles of the technological mosaic on which a business's – a country's or humankind's – strategy can base itself to win the challenge of sustainability?

In the beginning, there was *The Internet*

The rain was beating on the window pane. The wind was blowing the branches of the battered trees. At night, they made the little alley of that remote roman outskirt even gloomier. Valerio has been seated in his car for hours. He had always loved investigative journalism, but sometimes the stakeouts could be really dull. Finally, a shadow moved in the dark, getting closer to the front door he was watching. Despite the darkness, the outlines of that figure were unmistakable. There was no doubt. It was him—a paramount scoop. Eventually, the director would have noticed him and gave him the right place. Another shoot or two, and he was ready to send them straight to the newsroom. In a few minutes, social would have gone crazy over the news. A matter of minutes: going public meant being there before the conclusion of the ongoing negotiation.

He was fast taking those pictures. He was excited when he sent them to his smartphone to forward them to the editorial staff. Just then, his heart missed a beat—a cold shiver running through his spine. Disappointment and rage made him grit his teeth—the signal: the bloody mobile's signal. There was no signal. And there was no time to move before the negotiation was over. It was too late. His scoop was gone.

We do not know what Valerio's scoop was, nor who that person was on the threshold. We know for sure that timing was fundamental. It would have been fundamental if there had not been a common problem: the lack of a mobile signal. There is always the signal, other than when you need it.

The importance of being *online*

In Valerio's case, it was a missed scoop; in other cases, the impossibility to call a tow truck. The situations can be more serious, in which it is not possible to call an ambulance. Or situations not connected to a mobility condition. It is the case of a zone with no coverage and no access to the broadband network, forcing to make do with makeshift means. It is serious if you are a family. Seriously damaging if you are a factory, potentially devastating if you are a community.

In the always-on era – a condition that determines a model of services people got used to. This model consists of the possibility to access the Internet from everywhere and in every moment – we acknowledge the importance of being connected as a deduction: when it is not possible to be.

Those few seconds of isolation are enough to think about the central position of "connection" in our lives. This connection, for better or for worse, has already changed our habits and behaviors, reshaping the management of our primary activities: getting information and views of the world, being aware of what happens around us, building opinions on events and phenomena, making choices, getting to know other people, tying bonds, making friends, and also falling in love.

We could waste our time discussing if those changes were an advantage or a disadvantage for society, as, at the end of the Eighteenth Century, they debated whether the electric lightning in houses was useful, or the telephone, or the automobile mentioned above. No doubt, the web's pervasiveness is warping our society, and we need to keep it under control. Almost 20 years ago, Jeremy Rifkin postulated that "when everything around us is for sale, existence becomes the most sophisticated of the products and the economic sphere becomes the final judge of our personal and social life[101]." Time proved him to be right, as underlined by Jose Van Dijck[102] about 18 years later. He stigmatizes the risks of what he calls platforms society. He orients his reflections on the role of these big (economic, social, and relational) intermediation platforms in the community, underlining the potential warps and offering a total reshaping of their position.

---

[101] J. Rifkin, The Age Of Access:The New Culture of Hypercapitalism, Where All of Life Is a Paid-For Experience, 2001.

[102] J. Van Dijck, T. Poell, M. de Waal, *Platform Society: Public Values in a Connective World*, Oxford University Press, 2018.

However, it is essential to distinguish between the platforms mentioned by Van Dijck, that is to say, the big players that are now dictating the paradigm of the Net usage and the Net, in its profound nature, that is to say, the instrument used by the platform to reach the users. Too often, these two concepts are put together when it should be better to keep them separated:

- The Internet net, as a system to access the information and as a means of universal communication;
- The platforms based on the Net that use the access infrastructure to reach the users and offer the services.

This difference is relevant, considering that on the one hand, we talk about a free, open, and universal infrastructure; on the other, we talk about specific services offered by commercial operators with their (legitimate, but one-sided) goals.

It strikes as meaningful that the United Nations in 2012 declared access to the Internet and freedom of opinion and expression online to be fundamental rights[103]. They highlight the position of ITU – the UN's organization for telecommunication – already expressed in 2003[104]. According to the UN, "the same rights people have when they are off-line must be defended online, especially the freedom of expression applied beyond the boundaries and on every media."

That is why we need to look beyond the advantages and disadvantages of the Net itself. We need to contextualize its role not only related to change it triggered in society but also associated with the change we would like it to trigger. The direction of the development of the Net with its purely instrumental nature, on the basis of sustainable models and ideas.

---

[103] Resolution A/HCR/20/L.13

[104] World Summit on the Information Society. Geneve, 2003. *Declaration of Principles. Building the Information Society: a global challenge in the new millennium*, United Nations – ITU.

Vinton Cerf[105], one of the founding fathers of the web, underlined its instrumental nature. He declared: "There is a high bar for something to be considered a human right. Loosely put, it must be among the things we as humans need to lead healthy, meaningful lives, like freedom from torture or freedom of conscience. It is a mistake to place any particular technology in this exalted category since we will end up valuing the wrong things over time. For example, at one time, if you didn't have a horse, it was hard to make a living. In that case, the important right was the right to make a living, not the right to a horse. Today, if I were granted a right to have a horse, I'm not sure where I would put it[106]."
Vinton Cerf actually is not criticizing the concept of the Internet as a right, but he thinks it should be appropriate to consider it a civil right more than a human right: "The countries [...] have never decreed that everyone has a "right" to a telephone, we have come close to this with the notion of "universal service" – the idea that telephone service (and electricity, and now broadband Internet) must be available even in the most remote regions of the country. When we accept this idea, we are edging into the idea of Internet access as a civil right, because ensuring access is a policy made by the government." In other words, his warning is clear: we do not have to consider the Internet as an abstract right but as an instrument whose availability must be guaranteed by the Governments to carry out the fundamental rights of citizens.

This may not be a philosophical stance, but it is undoubtedly pragmatic. Let's look at digital transformation as an instrument for sustainability. We need to embrace this view, strongly underlining its instrumental function: it depends on private and public decision-makers' concrete choices.

---

[105] Vinton Gary Cerf, also known as Vint Cerf, is a celebrated American information scientist, he entered history as the "father of the Internet". He and Bob Kahn invented the protocols TCP/IP, a fundamental constitutive structure of the internet system as we know it. From 2005 he is Google's Chief Internet Evangelist. Amongst others, he won the Turing Award and the Presidential Medal for Freedom awarded by the President of The United States.

[106] V. G. Cerf, *Internet Access Is Not a Human Right*, New York Times, 24th January, 2002.

Why do we need the broadband?

The question may look trivial. It is enough to look at the scarce consideration the Italian government gave to the matter (compared to that of other countries) to understand how our decision-makers are plunged into an abyss of unawareness about the digital issues. If access to the Internet can and must be considered as a fundamental right, whether civil or human, then the broadband becomes functional to its usage.

The reason is straightforward: the amount of data traveling through the Web is increasing in geometric progression, and the services offered by the web need more space to be transmitted but also more stable, reliable, and safe networks. The old telephone twisted pair, the one for copper-wire networks, has had its chips. The optic-fiber cables are necessary because they enable processing a more significant amount of data per second compared to the copper-wires and also because they offer more excellent reliability, endurance, and easier maintenance—fast connection and reliability: two paramount factors for the Web to produce value.

To make it simple, the Internet is like a colossal waterwork in which we are pumping more and more water (the information we get on the Web) for more and more users every day. Our goal must be double: on the one hand, we must guarantee that the water pressure is adequate; on the other, we must ensure a rapid maintenance service. In both cases, old-generation technologies (such as the ADSL connection for homes) are inefficient. The risk of prolonging their usage is double: on the one hand, the risk is that the water arrives at low pressure when people need it the most (such as in the morning and at night when people wash. The same goes for Web traffic concentrated in particular moments of the day) on the other, the risk is a waterwork breakdown. broadband availability is fundamental to develop cutting-edge services: the services of essential importance transmitted online are more and more widespread. Reliability related to these services is crucial. Think about telehealth, the management system for Public Administration, corporate operating systems, surveillance applications, not to mention cutting-edge services connected to *smart* towns such as self-driving cars. In conclusion, the Web is – and will be – not only at the basis of our digital dimension but also at the foundation of society as a whole. In this framework, the distinction between real and virtual loses its meaning to make way to a reality dimension distinguished for its digital and analogic aspects. The availability of a broadband network is a real pre-condition.

The broadband between the fiber optics and 5G

Talking about network availability, we face the results of practical choices: how many investments in infrastructures should be made to ensure access to the Web for every citizen, every institution, and every enterprise? Which technologies do we need to aim for to guarantee the sustainability of the investments over time?
The answers are not simple. They influenced the role of entire Countries on Web development and affected those countries' ability to benefit from the dynamics of the digital transformation.

Our Country – take as example Valerio's story: he found himself with no signal in the Capital's outskirts – has brought up the rear in Europe for a very long time, in matters of Net diffusion and particularly broadband networks. The last positions occupied – with unenviable persistence – in the global rating and indexes about the spread of the broadband infrastructure for connection are due to historical reasons. The neverending *querelle* concerning the unbundling[107] engendered a delay in the development of the optic-fiber-cabled infrastructure. This fact produced an infrastructural *digital divide*, facilitating the development of another dangerous *digital divide*: the cultural *digital divide*. It is clear that if the networks are underdeveloped, the users will hardly develop a culture for their correct usage[108]. This combined outcome of the two digital divides – infrastructural and cultural – produced a general delay in the Country's ability

---

[107] With the term unbundling we refer to the partition of the physical infrastructure from the other business activities of the telecommunication industries (landline telephony, mobile telephony, internet, and media). In Italy Telecom Italia, now TIM, holds the physical network infrastructure. This division and reorganization of the network would guarantee the "neutrality", simplyfing the access to the new landline operators and to the Internet.

[108] Concering the human capital, Italy is in the 26th position out of 28 Countries of the European Union. The level of the basic digital expertise is way under the Eurpoean average level: only 44% of people between 16 and 74 possess the basic digital knowledge

to take advantage of the digital possibilities. This delay affected the GPD rate[109]and will have more significant impacts in the future if our decision-makers do not give relevance to the matter.

The role of 5G technology to face and solve the digital divide problem in Italy is widely discussed. To deal appropriately with this matter, we need to be careful: we must not generalize. 5G technology will indeed have a revolutionary impact on dozens of sectors. It will help reshape the enterprises: from the automotive industry to the health service from the entertainment to the agroindustry. However, the development of 5G, for which Italy is a cutting-hedge country[110], is not enough to solve *tout court* the problem of deficiency for cabled-network infrastructures. Because 5G is a wireless technology, but the transceiver antennas on which it is based need to be connected to a cabled network. Thus, the development of the 5G does not overlook the cabled network's adaptation, which is a fundamental pre-condition for the development of this revolutionary technology.

As it happened for the optic fiber and the copper wire, the advantages of 5G compared to the previous generations of transmission systems for mobility data are not only connected to the speed of the connection, even if it will be one thousand times faster than the present (to talk numbers: with 5G it will take about 30 seconds to download a two-and-a-half-last-

---

(57% in the EU). The percentage of ITC specialist in factories is 2.6%, the EU average is 3.7%. Only 1% of the Italians has a degree in ITC. Only 1% of working women is in the ITC sector. As for digital competenc, from 2005 on, only 20% of teachers attended continuing education courses for the digital knowledge and 24% of schools lack programming courses. Furthermore, in 2018, 19% of the Italian population had never used the Internet, only 46% ever used online banking, 47% has made online purchaces and only 11% of enterprises has online shops. [source: DESI, National Report for 2019, Italy].

[109] According to Digital Advisory Group of the American Chamber of Commerce in Italy. The impact of the digital divide could reach 4% of the GPD.

[110] Pre-commercial experimentations in three geographic areas have been made, with usage tests. Other tests have been made on the basis of agreements between the municipalities and the operators in Rome, Turin, Naples, and Genua. In Italy 94% of the spectrum harmonization for the wireless broadband has been set. [source: DESI, National Report for 2019, Italy].

ing movie in ultra-high-resolution). In fact, the other two fundamental elements come into play: the number of connected devices and the quickness of the answer.

Concerning the number of connected devices, about a million per square kilometer[111], the connection will develop new services on the Internet of thing vision. In other words, it will be possible to connect every object to the Net, interacting in real-time.
The quickness of the answer is a different factor. I can have a tap pumping one thousand liters per second, but it takes a minute to open fully. 5G will take less than a millisecond to open that tap.

The number of connected devices, the quickness of the answer, together with the speed of the connection, will lay the foundation for a real change of standars in dozens of sectors.

The broadband for sustainability

Unlike other technologies, when we talk about broadband, it is not easy to link this tile of the digital transformation to specific elements of sustainability or fixed goals of sustainable development. The broadband is necessary infrastructure, diagonal to all the targets set by Agenda 2030. Without broadband, there is no Net; without the Net, there is no possibility to develop digital transformation processes. That is why investing in the building of reliable and high-performance broadband infrastructures – such as the 5G and the optic fiber – is the pre-condition to every argument about the advantages of digital transformation for sustainability.
The availability of the band will enable the services to make our towns and territories *smart*. Thanks to the objects' constant connection to the Net, the territories will be able to supply innovative services close to the citizens. The band availability enables the most advanced applications of artificial intelligence, thanks to which we will create flexible and efficient digital instruments able to cooperate with human beings in their

---

[111] International Telecomunication Union ITU, *Draft new Report ITU-R M.[IMT-2020.TECH PERF REQ] - Minimum requirements related to technical performance for IMT-2020 radio interface(s)*, ITU public document, 2017.

primary activities: the driving of vehicles (*self-driving cars*), the management of the electricity (*smart grid*), the support in complex surgical operations (*smart surgery*), the cooperation with the decision-makers in the strategic choices for the future of a territory *(data-driven governance)*.

Mapping out the Net's role in the targets of Agenda 2030, it is clear how it touches all the goals having infrastructure as a pivotal element.

Thanks to the Internet and the broadband, we can:

- Have access to education device, even in the remotest areas of the globe (**goal 4:** Ensure inclusive and equitable quality education and promote lifelong learning opportunities for all)
- Contribute to the development of culture and knowledge, demolishing all discriminations and reaching gender equality reducing social inequality (**Goal 5**:Achieve gender equality and empower all women and girls **Goal 10**: Reduce inequality within and among countries)
- Promote the development of a healthy economy, caring about the workers and the resources (**Goal 8**: Promote sustained, inclusive and sustainable economic growth, full and productive employment and decent work for all; **Goal 9**: Build resilient infrastructure, promote inclusive and sustainable industrialization and foster innovation; Goal 12: Ensure sustainable consumption and production patterns;)
- Support the development of human-friendly towns **Goal11:** Make cities and human settlements inclusive, safe, resilient, and sustainable)
- Contribute to the creation of a better society thanks to the building of bridges between different cultures and shared sustainable development patterns (**goal 16:** Promote peaceful and inclusive societies for sustainable development, provide access to justice for all and build effective, accountable, and inclusive institutions at all levels; **goal 17**: Strengthen the means of implementation and revitalize the global partnership for sustainable development).

In conclusion, the Net is – and will be, if we know how to use it – an instrument of freedom, social, economic, and environmental welfare.

Cloud computing: the services in a cloud

The availability of an always-on connection and a widespread and better computing power enabled the development of new service patterns that changed the relationship between digital devices and their users. Amongst the services patterns, the most relevant is cloud computing.
The base concept of cloud computing is not so complicated[112]; although it is now a consolidated means of service distribution, conceptually, it is unknown to many people. At the dawning of the Net, each computer was accessible through a specific address. Because of the growing number of users, it would have been impossible for a single computer – no matter how powerful – to manage all the requests simultaneously. The client-server model was showing its limits. A new approach developed, based on the fact that each client's claim was not addressed to a single computer but to an indistinct group of computers that answered – overall – a single address. A "cloud" of computers, at the users' service. In this way, the interconnected computers could balance the traffic and answer the users' requests efficiently.

This service pattern, together with a greater fastness of the nets and the possibility to develop a continuous data stream between the user's computer and the cloud of remote computers, allowed to use the cloud not only to host internet websites but also to supply more and more sophisticated services similar – in features and graphic interface – to those managed on the user's terminal.

Word processors, spreadsheets, presentation templates can be accessible by remote, that is, without installing them on the computer (the same that happens when a user checks his mailbox without a *client* on his computer but using a *browser*). The software has always been considered something to be uploaded on the client's computer, but now it becomes an online service. It is the SaaS pattern: Software as a Service. A real revolution for the software industry and all the users as well.

---

[112] As an example we mention the *Innovation as a development lever: entrepreneurs' point of view* Survey, made in 2018 by the Digitald Transformation Institute. It states that one entrepreneur out of three knows the concept of cloud computing, even if using services supplied through this modality

"To remote" the software products, transforming them into services allowed to simplify the usage of these instruments, because it is unnecessary to know how to use a computer in its advanced features such as settings, security management, and updating. A web connection is enough to use the most updated and complex services without installing them on the PC.

There is also the other side of the coin: using cloud software means to relinquish all the private information and personal data. Opting for a cloud provider – operators that provide services in cloud mode – implies trusting these operators, handling all the complex management activities, and all the user's information. This is a condition to be aware of. It is also necessary to consider all the potential consequences of what is called *lock-in*[113], that is, the difficulty, once chosen a cloud solution, to change the operator.

C*loud computing* for sustainability

As we said about connectivity, the cloud, as well, has a diagonal function towards the goals of Agenda 2030, being an enabling technology. However, it is possible to identify some vertical elements regarding the topic of sustainability.

In general, resorting to cloud computing fosters the development of service platforms dedicated to managing specific functions, reducing the complexity of the systems' implementation.

In other words, it would be unreasonable for Anna to implement, in her factory, all the necessary functions for the management of her complex

[113] For enterprises we talk about lock-in when they invested in technologies below their expectations, but it is expensive to get out of the investment. This difficulty is given by the investment's fixed costs, that would be lost, or by net externalities amongst enterprises using the same technology. That is why a change to another standard must be accepted by all of them. This case is not about money, but it deals with a coordination issue amongst the factories operating in that market. In general technological lock-in allows the "creation of boundaries, when joining, towards potential competitors and the acquisition of power in the market." [source: Treccani Encyclopedia.]

systems. The control sensors in her stables, the webcams for her cattle, the product tracking system, the clients' loyalty process require vertical expertise for management and maintenance, which would transform Anna's cheese factory into a software house. Resorting to cloud systems releases Anna from the management issues connected to the software, allowing her to use products and applications that otherwise would be a big industries' prerogative. This element matches the spirit of **Goal 8:** *Promote sustained, inclusive, and sustainable economic growth, full and productive employment, and decent work for all.* And also matches most of its targets[114].

The cloud achieves the reduction of the complexity of the services' management. When combined with information distribution models based on open data (public data openly distributed[115]), it achieves sharing and standardization. Information sharing and standardization allow better usage and also to orientate them towards sustainable development and

---

[114] In particular:

- Target 8.2: Achieve higher levels of economic productivity through diversification, technological upgrading and innovation, including through a focus on high-value added and labour-intensive sectors. The adoption of the cloud is an updating element enhancing factories' productivness.
- Target 8.3: Promote development-oriented policies that support productive activities, decent job creation, entrepreneurship, creativity and innovation, and encourage the formalization and growth of micro-, small- and medium-sized enterprises, including through access to financial services. The adoption of the cloud allows the SMSE to be competitive, otherwise they would risk being thrown out of the market.
- Target 8.8: Protect labour rights and promote safe and secure working environments for all workers, including migrant workers, in particular women migrants, and those in precarious employment. The adoption of the cloud allows the standardization of behaviors connected to the regulations that impose on the factories standard procedures.

[115] Open data (information, numerical data, etc.) can be freely used more than once, redistributed according to the terms of service. The data are made available and usable by means of a standard-open format, readable by a computing application. All of this to make it easier for third parties to access and reuse the data and release them through royalty-free-licences. Open data are the result of internal processes made by factories or public administration and their free distribution allow the development of new and empowered appllications and services. Globally, the outline of the standard and patterns is provided by the Open Knowledge Foundation, founded by Rufus Pollock and Cathrine Stihler.

consumption patterns, as stated by **Goal 12:** *Ensure sustainable consumption and production patterns.* The enhancement of cloud-based solutions allows the achievement – with adequate standardization – of optimized chains of value. In the light of sustainability, this can produce savings and a real decrease in wastefulness. That is the case of *Food.Cloud.* It is an Irish organization that developed a *cloud* platform interfacing with the supermarkets' storage management, intercepting the potential stock surplus. In accord with the supermarket's store manager, this surplus can be directed to the charities supporting the poor.
These charities are connected to Food.Cloud. The outcomes are striking: by optimizing the supermarkets' storehouse, one single organization could distribute 65 million meals, an average of 37 meals per minute 24/7. Thanks to the spread in England and Ireland, it supplied 27 thousand tons of food, with an 80 million euros value and a saving of 87 thousand CO_2 tons, matching entirely **Goal 13:** *Take urgent action to combat climate change and its impacts.*

The question is clear and inevitable: if a single organization, thanks to the cloud computing technology and win-win pattern, was able to obtain such good outcomes through implementation of such a simple service, what would happen if the companies' willpower, after a collective reflection, should be oriented towards the exploitation of the available technologies to develop a sustainable future?
To say it in other words, what would happen if the world started to think in terms of (digital) sustainability?

The *social network site* and the age of platforms

If Carla had a euro for each broken stethoscope, she would have been rich. Every time she was lost in her thoughts, she couldn't help fiddling with it. The result, no matter its resistance, was always the same. Crack.

Over the last 200 years, the stethoscope hadn't changed so much: that's why she had it always on her. Like a necklace. She loved to think that, in a job that was changing fast, it was constant.

After all, one needed anchorage. When she got her degree, the world was different. Today everything was changing: technologies, therapies, even relationships with patients. Thinking about this last point had started a series of reflections that now were endangering the umpteenth unfortunate tool.

At the end of her working day, she used to allow herself a little break. She opened Facebook to have a look at her friend's posts. She felt a bit ashamed, but after all, it relieved her day.

The request was there. Waiting for her to decide. She had met Maria two days ago in her study: a sorrowful look, a build that bore the signs of a severe eating disorder, clearly visible even in her profile picture. Now she was staring at her, with her big eyes, magnified by the leanness of her face.

She used Facebook to relax, and her job followed her even there. This was annoying. She needed a place for herself, after all. Maybe, she couldn't help thinking, for girls like Maria, social networks were more than a pastime. They were a part of their world. And that friend request was actually a help request. What to do? She had already decided. She didn't want to abandon her, nor all the others.

And while she was confirming Maria's request, she felt under her fingertips the umpteenth crack. Another stethoscope was gone.

And maybe the place for herself was gone too.

Is she doing the right thing to confirm her patients' friends requests on Facebook or any other social network site? In general: is it a good thing for a physician to interact with his patients out of his study or out of his professional duty, letting them enter the apparent "private" sphere of social media? And again: is she aware that, the moment they become "virtual" friends, she starts setting an example with her behaviors? Is she able to behave like a model, or at least to understand that all of her actions are public communication on the Net?

These are not common questions, and there is not a right or wrong answer. These questions concern a lot of people. Physicians have a particular role, but it is the same for lawyers, teachers, law enforcement agents, not to mentions judges. Or referees...

The Internet, thus, is changing completely the way people get their information, but above all, people's relationships, the way they make friends. This change alters not only the "how" dimension, opening new, unexplored relational spaces but also the "what" dimension. It is redefining the meaning of relationship that – acting in an original dynamic torn between the analogic and the digital contexts – is evolving in different directions, challenging to foresee, but fundamental to examine.

Real and virtual

Social network sites such as Facebook, Twitter, and their epigones, are the arrival point of a long development path.

When Tim Berner-Lee conceived the Web, he had in mind a model to share information amongst researchers. The focus was on the content more than the building of relationships between the content provider. The goal was mainly the creation of a system to assist the scientists' cooperation. However, this model was so simple and efficient that it took hold vehemently outside its birth context. From the beginning, the growth of websites was massive. The first website, realized by Tim Berners-Lee, was born in 1991[116]. In 1993 there were only 130 websites, but in 1997 they were over a million already, to reach 17 million in 2000. In 2016 active websites were over a billion, and today they are almost 2 billion[117].

A fundamental step in this path was in 1997 when Dave Winer realized the first software to build a *"blog."* This term is the contraction of the expression *web log*. A trace left by the users to share with other people reflections and travel notes.

Blogs are just users' managed sites, led by the need to share their experiences. They can do that thanks to simple instruments of automatic publishing as simple as a word processor: the CMS.[118]
If the web is the internet's killer application, then blogs are a fundamental transition for the information world in general. Thanks to them, the concept of User Generated Content (UGC) is born. They are users' generated contents that demolish the wall between producers and information users so that in 2006 The Times chose to award the Person's of the Year price – with a very symbolic choice – to the user himself, as a real protagonist of the information world.[119]
It has been a decade since that article, and the impacts of that historic change still echo in the complex debates about the information world's evolutions after the processes of digital transformation.

The blog is a revolutionary social media[120]. We even talk about web 2.0[121]to define a new way to look at the web. A web based on concepts such as decentralization, openness, participation, and cooperation, the lack of

---

[116] Tim Berners-Lee publishes the first website on the 6th August 1991. The first visit to the site was made the following 23rd August. [Source: The birth of the Web]

[117] Source: Internet Live Stats

[118] Content Management System

[119] The Time's reason is particularly meaningful: it published a cover with a sentence appearing on a screen: "YOU" "yes, you control the information age. Welcome to your world"

[120] According to Andreas Kaplan and Michael Haenlein social media are a group of Internet-based applications, built on the ideological and technological principles of Web 2.0, enabling the creation and exchange of users generated contents.

[121] Term created by Tim O'Reilly in 2004.

any barrier between the content-makers and the users[122]. The blog and the web 2.0, in conclusion, embody the highest moment for the Net as a symbol of an open, free, and cooperating system. This meaning is going to change over the years, betrayed and withdrawn by the so-called platform society.

We get close to the platforms society thanks to the social network sites: a particular kind of social media based on platforms' ability to track the relationships among the users through a social graph[123]. This graph codifies their contacts, their activities, their preferences. The management platforms on which the social network sites are based - thanks to techniques such as social network analysis[124] and big data analysis[125] - can precisely understand the users' characteristics and tastes, creating value according to this information, inferred by their behaviors. The business channel is mainly that of advertising. The platforms are also experimenting with other value-making channels[126].

Apart from these fundamental considerations about the platforms and the way they use to create value, taking it from the users' actions

---

[122] To better understand the role and impacts of social media on the social relationships patterns see A. Marinelli COnnessioni, Nuovi Media, nouve relazioni sociali (Connections, New Media, new social relationships), Guerini Editore, 2005.

[123] A social graph is a visual representation of a social network, describing a community of individuals (the "knots" of the web) and their connections (the "arches").

[124] When we talk about Social Network Analysis (SNA) we refer to a pattern used to analize the social relationships between individuals and groups of people, using mathematics and statistics. The goal is to map, according to quantity and quality, the networks sprung from the social ties between individuals. The social network analysis developed thanks to the Austrian psychiatrist and father of the sociomerty, Jacob Levi Moreno.

[125] The big data analysis' purpose is to analyse a big amount of data, differing from type, nature, and structure underlining the relevant inferences.

[126] The main social network sites are engaged in the development of alternative profit systems, connected not only to targeted advertising. It is interesting for example the use made by Instagram of the "interactive" posts, enabling the user to tag the products in the pictures, and to make a purchase with a few clicks. Again, Facebook is changing the pages into real market places, offering products and services; furthermore, thanks to the augmented reality, it is creating captivating games and products available in its platform.

(whether they are aware or not), it is clear that the first platforms, Facebook above all, led to the destruction of the barrier between "real" and "virtual."

Those with gray hair surely remember Second Life: a pioneering and forgotten platform based on immersive virtual reality. The user is represented by an avatar[127] and moves, exploring a fantasy world, dwelled by other avatars, behind which there are other users.
The peculiar feature of Second Life is the representation of an ideal second life. In this sense, Second Life is a good picture of the social contexts developing during the first years of the Net. The net of the Usenet[128], or before the Internet age of the Fidonet[129]. Online contacts were destined to stay online. The concept of "virtual" expresses a divide related to "real" life. Second life gives the chance to live a second, virtual life, separated from the first, real life, the everyday life with its contacts.

Facebook tears down this barrier. It is a social network site, and it builds its value through the tracking of users' relationships and their contents, but the fundamental feature of Mark Zuckerberg's system is to remove the wall between real and virtual relationships. On Facebook, It is easy to create a fake account; it is true. However, the rates are relatively low[130] related to the total number of active users in the platform, and the majority is not created by ordinary users[131]. Most active users do not see Facebook as a context in which living a second life, but only as an extension of the relational patterns used in daily life. On Facebook, you do not have

---

[127] The term "avatar" comes from the Sanskrit and means the incarnation of the divine, or in broad sense, the ideal being.

[128] Acronym of user network, a computer network used to share worldwide discussion forums dedicated to specific topics.

[129] Fidonet was a BBS net (bulletin board system) worldwide spred. Computers were connected to the telephone network and a complex messaging exchange protocol enabling in a few days the computers connected to the net to share the contents produced by the users. This net was created in 1984 by Tom Jennings.

[130] The percentage of fake accounts on Facebook in 2009 was between 3% and 5% of the total.

[131] The majority of the fake accounts is created by professionists for different reasons: from the spread of fake news to the marketing. The creation of fake account is not allowed by the social networks' policy, once signalled by the other users, the fake account is cancelled.

virtual friends, you communicate with friends of the first (and only) life. Mark Zuckerberg's social media was the first platform to reach that critical number of people to trigger positive net externalities[132], that is, those dynamics according to which the more people join the platform, the more the platform becomes useful for the users[133]. And for the managers, of course.

Regardless of facebook's destiny, this social media was the first to allow the development of a relational continuity (and contiguity) between what we used to call virtual reality and real space. Today we can talk about a digital and physical dimension of relationships, part of the same reality, determined by online moments and off-line moments.

It is too soon to understand what these impacts caused and will cause on relationships; leaving out ideologies and the pathological[134] dimension, it is clear that they will produce a retroaction in how people build their connections and also how they manage their time.

Carla's question of whether to confirm or not her patients on Facebook arises from this: the social network sites tore down the wall between real and virtual, contaminating reality with a digital dimension and carrying it in the Net. How much is it going to affect human relations? How much is it going to make the relations shallower? How much is the disintermediation of the physical dimension contributing to the demolition of the relational barriers? How is the very concept of friendship going to change? We are experiencing a cause-effect reversal. In the past, one used to spend some time with someone before calling him a friend. Now, confirming a friendship is the first step to get to know someone. We are facing a real anthropological change; we have barely grasped its magnitude. We can fear it and try (in vain?) to escape. Or we can try and understand

---

[132] Carl. Shapiro, *Information rules: a strategic guide to the network economy*, Harvard Business Press, 1999.

[133] B. Belvaux, *The Development of Social Media: Proposal for a Diffusion Model Incorporating Network Externalities in a Competitive Environment*, Recherche et Applications en Marketing, 2011.

[134] IAD – Internet Addiction Disorder, it is classified amongst the addictions such as drug and alcohol.

it to develop the right antibodies for the problems it will bring about, but also try and seize the advantages.

Relation and content

Social network sites contributed to tearing down the wall between the real and the virtual (in its essence, even before common perception), and also, they marked the transition from the content age to the relation age.

The blog's features dictated (and dictate, the means has not disappeared) the formation of structured contents. In other words, to share a post[135], it has to make sense. This depends on the structure of this means: the blog is made of brief articles written by the author (the posts). The contents' quality determines the blog's worth, the prestige (and reputation) of the blogger.

The development of social network sites shifted the ground by changing the nature of the means. These instruments tend to make the sharing action as simple as it can be. Each sharing corresponds to an enrichment of the social graph connected to the social network site. And every graph's enrichment corresponds to the platform's empowerment to understand the user that shared something. In other words, every time we put a *like,* every time we write a reply, every time we choose to follow a page, every time we ask a friendship, we are saying something about ourselves to the platform. Something that will help it to get to know us.

Facebook and the other social network sites can potentially track Maria's eating disorder as fast as Carla. By analyzing her behaviors, by the pages she visits, by the pictures she comments on. To get to know its users, the platform encourages them to share, relate to each other, show what they like and don't. By making interactions as easy as possible. The axis shifts from the writing of contents – long and difficult to organize – to the sharing of state of mind, feelings, emotions, replies.

---

[135] A post is the minimal unit of content in a blog. It can be compared to a newspaper's article.

We could say that blogs are about content, social network sites are about relations. On the one hand, the social graph thickens, allowing the platforms to get to know its users (and extract the value efficiently); on the other, it impoverishes the net and its contents.

Users write less but connect more to other users and to what they like. This tendency is underlined by the evolution – not by chance – of the social networking instruments that push their sharing functions towards the usage promptness.

The impoverishment of contents is just one of the side effects produced by this "sharing coaction" typical of the platforms. Platforms' goal is to get to know their users; the best way to achieve this goal is to increase the time the user spends on the platform and spend time on the platform the user needs to be at ease. That is why the platforms encourage – employing ad-hoc algorithms – the natural human inclination to relate with people sharing the same opinions[136]. This tendency is highlighted by the social media walled garden, a shelter for people to feel comfortable and stay on the platform as long as possible. This tendency runs the risk of developing what Eli Pariser called the "filter bubble.[137]" Filter bubbles engender the user's enclosure inside a real ideological frame[138], giving him a vision of the world fitting with his point of view, hiding the differences, and altering his perception of the diversity.

Out of any critics, this phenomenon allows the transmission of the so-called *fake news*, false news.
People, accustomed to seeing what they want to see and not prone to confrontation, closed in their filter bubble, give for granted that what they receive on their timeline is the truth and –considering it under their perspective – decide to share it without thinking. There is some more: they believe what they read to be accurate, and not seeing any contrasting

[136] In Social Network Analysis this characteristic is called homophilia and it is based on two effects: contamination effect, which leads people to behave like their counterpart, and the wave effect which leads people to behave like the ones surrounding them.

[137] E. Parisier, The Filter Bubble: What The Internet Is Hiding From You, Penguin Books Limited, 2011

[138] Jacob Weisberg

opinion thanks to the filter bubble, they favor the plausible fact over the true and verified. They hear what they want to hear. In a context where people are focused on the same point of view, no one cares if a piece of information is accurate or to be verified. Plausibility is enough. This phenomenon is defined as *post truth*[139]. This fact was not born with the internet, but it thrives thanks to the internet and social media. It is impossible to cope with it on technical and legislative grounds but a cultural ground, as we said in the Fake News Manifesto edited by the Digital Transformation Institute.[140]

Social network sites for sustainability

Filter bubbles, post truth, fake news. The menu is not appealing. We need to remember that this menu, innate in human relationships, is just a part of the whole, and social network sites are just a powerful catalyst, but not a generating factor.

This whole, going back to Carla's story, leads Maria in a tunnel in which everyone needs to be tragically thin, but also it allows her to exit the walled garden (that is not created by the social media) and ask for Carla's help. Of course, it's up to Carla to decide how to behave. Again it is a matter of choice. She can choose to keep a professional relationship with her patient, inside her study, or – following a new arduous path – to use the instruments at her disposal and use the Net, formerly a pastime, for a higher purpose. It refers to **Goal 3:** Ensure healthy lives and promote well-being for all at all ages.[141]

Carla can choose to help Maria, and also she can decide to support the distribution of quality content by contrasting the fake news in the medical field, promoting rightful information. Maybe by breaking the echo-

---

[139] According to the Oxford Dictionary the term was created by Steve Tesich.

[140] Appendix 5: Fake News Manifesto,the Digital Transformation Institute published in 2017.

[141] We refer specifically to **Target 3.4** : by 2030, reduce by one third premature mortality from non-communicable diseases through prevention and treatment and promote mental health and well-being.

chambers,[142]developing around sided and prejudicial positions to try and bring back people to more open-minded visions and face confrontation. Through confrontation, helping them rediscover the value of competence. It is worth underlining that in Carla's case, her choice is not merely an individual action; in a broader context, it can be considered a real system action. It is what has been made by HealthUnlocked, a social network site born in Great Britain, to link professionals, health organizations, and patients on a single platform. This platform now counts about 40 million users all over the world, and its purpose is to create online communities focused on giving information and support to members sharing the same diseases, with the help of institutions and health professionals present on the platform. In this sense, social media are a powerful instrument with significant impact. The same patterns used to create fake news should be employed to broadcast-quality content; this is not only possible but also represents the best weapon to fight misinformation on the Web.

The achievement of this goal is essential worldwide, but in some areas – because of economic and social development conditions – it is utterly irreplaceable. An interesting case is that of Malawi, where UNICEF developed a multiplatform system, integrating a website, social media, and the old but still used SMSs to sensibilize the population, especially girls, about gender violence topics and early marriages[143]. The users can access accurate information about their rights through different channels, and they can also contact, through the same channels, lawyers, psychologists, and support communities. An excellent way to fulfill **Goal 5:** Achieve gender equality and empower all women and girls. It is particularly incisive because it uses the same communication channels used by girls and potential users, and the anonymity is a guarantee against retaliation. In terms of knowledge as an instrument for economic growth and respect for human rights, DigitalGreen, active in India, Ghana, and Ethiopia, is

---

[142] With this expression we mean a spread condition according to which every individual is offered information and content that, regadless of any accuracy, relevance, or truthfulness matches their "tastes" or interests. The algorithms are made to satisfy, by contents'relevance criteria, the need for "confirmation" innate in every human being. The risk is to expose people to a warped perception of the social context, an echo of their point of view. An interesting analyses on the matter is reported in S. Kumar, N. Shah, False Information on Web and Social Media: A Survey, 1th April 2018.

[143] Unicef annual report, 2017, Malawi.

working on **Goal 4:** Ensure inclusive and equitable quality education and promote lifelong learning opportunities for all. The project was started by an Ong, financed by Bill and Melinda Gates Foundation, Google, and many other donors. It is based on a social network. Its purpose is to share videos and educate the local agricultural businessmen about their rights and the new farming techniques using an effective and simple instrument. The videos are made on the choices and preferences of the farmers who participate in the social network site activities. The farmers can join the online activities and in-site meetings, where they are displayed through laptops. These meetings are realized for those who have no access to the Web: we need to bear in mind that connection is not granted in some areas. This is a virtuous example, showing that it is possible to work both with the digital and analogic dimensions, complementing each other, and also that the usage of online videos is not a TikTok[144] influencers' prerogative; on the other hand, videos can have a central role in the education and competence-building for all levels of population, all over the world.

Even more: unlike what happens with mass communication instruments, the social network sites allow us to divide the users and identify specific targets. This has been made by Amsterdam's Public Health Service to manage the sensibilization campaign on the diagnosis and testing of hepatitis C.[145] By using Facebook's segmentation instruments, it realized a categorized advertising campaign, customized according to specific risk profiles, inferred thanks to the users' online behaviors. In the end, the user was asked to fill an anonymous test to infer the possibility of contamination. People at a high-risk level decided to contact the Health Service. The use of the social network sites allowed a considerable cost reduction and also the possibility of reaching people otherwise impossible to identify, contributing to the fulfillment of Goal 3.

The social network sites as instruments:

- To foster dialogue and confrontation;

[144] TikTok is a social network developed in China by the ByteDance and released, in a first version, at the end of 2016. TikTok allows, by an app, to upload short videos with background music to share with other users. In Italy it is used by almost 2.5 million people, mostly teenagers and children.

[145] For more information visit WHO website.

- To support the awareness of human rights;
- To build competence through new information channels

But this is not enough. These instruments are sources that can be used for projects aimed at the analysis of data, useful to comprehend dynamics, dimensions, and diffusion of large-scale phenomena. Every action of the user is saved and can create value for the platform. In fact, according to who manages the platform, a piece of information can be available in a free (and of course anonymous) format. That is the case of the project realized by UNHCR[146] . With the UN Global Pulse's competence[147], it uses the social network, Twitter, particularly to identify models useful to trace the possible cross-border movements of migrants. The system is supported by big data analysis techniques and identifies, reads, and classifies geo-referenced tweets in specific geographic areas, written in different languages. The goal is to understand the migrants' movement. Their comments and replies and those of the people they meet in the countries they cross. We will have a powerful fact-finding instrument to develop a proper support policy. Social network sites and big data analysis are useful to achieve **Goal 10:** Reduce inequality within and among countries.[148]

It is also important to underline the role of social network sites to achieve **Goal 8:** *Promote sustained, inclusive and sustainable economic growth, full and productive employment and decent work for all.* These instruments have reshaped the way factories address the customers enabling new relational channels. The new dynamics are giving the platform a high power. Still, on the other hand, they are also allowing small businesses to go beyond the geographical limits and open themselves to the international markets, supporting their growth. In a context where most people spend several hours online, especially on these platforms, it is essential for survival that industries supervise them, but they are also a great opportunity.

---

[146] United Nations High Commissioner for Refugees

[147] It is a UN's project for the use of big data to achieve the goals of Agenda 2030.

[148] In particualr **Target 10.7**: Facilitate orderly, safe, regular and responsible migration and mobility of people, including through the implementation of planned and well-managed migration policies

Filter bubbles, post truth, fake news. Social network sites are all about this. These instruments monitor our lives. But they can also be free information, openness, education, awareness, cooperation, support. Once again, we are facing a choice. An individual choice, because the proper use depends on the knowledge of these instruments' characteristics. But also a collective choice because the approaches we will use to deal with the platforms in the future, on a political, institutional, and economic level, will define their role in the world. Whether it will be like for the Arab Spring (with some doubts on the effective role) or a sort of creepy surveillance society, it will rest on us. Once again, the future depends not only on the development of technology but also on our ability to orient it in the right direction[149].

Which role for platforms?

It is not wrong to ask ourselves if social media will disclose new relational scenarios or leave men on their own. Neither if they embody freedom and awareness contexts, or if they are control instruments. However, it is more fruitful to keep in mind that the answer rests on us. We need to ask ourselves how it is possible to orient them towards the first direction producing a positive impact on society. The question is vital because the role of these systems in our lives is central. These systems belong to many actors basing their business models on the ability to build value by extracting information out of the customers. Social networks such as Facebook, web browsers such as Google, and e-commerce systems such as Amazon – even if offering different services – have similar value-making models. They are based on extracting the value from the users' activities inside the platform and building it, starting from the information they can deduce from these activities.

This is the basis of what Alex Moazed and Nicholas Johnson define as "platform economy,"[150] that is to say, an economy based on the actors that

---

[149] L.Riccio, Un tweet non fa primavera. Il ruolo dei social media nella prmavera araba, dialoghi Mediterranei, 2007 (A tweet does not make a summer. The role of social media in the Arab Spring)

[150] A. Moazed, N. L. Johnson, *Modern Monopolies: What It Takes to Dominate the 21st-Century Economy*, St. Martin's Press, 2016.

"do not control the means of production, but they create means of connection and establish their meaning." This economy redefines the balance of power amongst the market actors, overturning consolidated logic, and submitting new important questions to society.
Never before, we dealt with actors capable of entering so profoundly inside people's lives. Platforms have access to such a significant number of data about their users and can analyze them with such efficient techniques to know more than the users think. They know more about the users than the users themselves. Every time we make an action online, this action says something about us. Every behavior depicts us. Every choice connotes us. Platforms can control the actions, analyze our behaviors, know our choices. On this basis, they outline a profile for each user. This profile not only describes what the user does but also deduces what he would do, what he would like, what he would choose.

In other terms, the platforms' business model, the system through which they increase their income, is based on identifying a user's profile as accurately as possible to create value on it and through it. As for social network sites and web browsers, this applies to their ability to send targeted advertising and also to identify the best solutions for the purchase of products and services. The most important capital for platforms is not made of means of production or physical infrastructures, nor of what they sell. The real value for realities such as Amazon or Alibaba is not the product on sale, but the users' knowing. This knowledge allows them to orientate the purchase towards the most plausible options based on the deduced tastes; enables them to manage the storehouses through refined analysis techniques, setting the stock on the basis of purchase previsions. Even the price is established on the analysis of the user's tendency and spending power.

The platforms' enormous power is evident. The ongoing attention towards the capture of data, the inclination to transform the deduced information into negotiable raw material, and the capacity to select the users on the basis of this information are the foundation of what we can call the platform society.[151] According to the authors of the namesake book,

---

[151] J. van Dijck, T. Poell, M. de Waal, *Platform Society*, Oxford University Press, 2018.

the platform society will require the definition of new rules by the institutions to guarantee the protection of the users' rights, which are and will be superimposable to the total of citizens.
We need new criteria and shared choices to avoid that the platform society turns into real surveillance capitalism:[152] based on a global surveillance structure according to which the apocalyptic vision described in Orwell's 1984[153] is just an optimistic interpretation of our probable future.

On the one hand, we are concerned about the possible deviations of platform capitalism; on the other hand, we postulate a future based on opposite concepts. They do not consider the platforms to be potential digital Panopticons[154]; instead, they believe them to be open and shared cooperation instruments.

It is what we call platform cooperativism[155], based on the principle that it is possible to develop a social and economic ecosystem, built on different models than those of the big for-profit corporations, controlling the Web and thriving on the alleged cooperation between equals—alleged, because too often, the value extracted from the users is not given back through services and other modalities in an equal measure. Platform cooperativism is based on principles focused on the values of equity, the acknowledgment of labor, the right to organize your own data. And last but not least, the possibility to disconnect, if willing to do so. The web envisaged by platform cooperativism does not see the platforms as famished giants, eager to devour their users' data. They are actors owned by the users themselves, based on an approach distributed to property. It takes its inspiration from the cooperative model and uses it to build a cutting-edge platform model.

---

[152] S. Zuboff, *Il capitalismo della sorveglianza. Il futuro dell'umanità nell'era dei nuovi poteri*,(surveillance capitalism. The future of humanity in the age of the new powers) Luiss University Press, 2019.

[153] G. Orwell, 1984, Secker & Warburg, London, 1948

[154] Panopticon is an ideal prison planned in 1791 by Jeremy Benthlam, an English philosopher and jurist. The concept is to allow a single jailer to monitor all the prisoners without being seen by them.

[155] T. Scholz, *Platform Cooperativism: Challenging the Corporate Sharing Economy*, Rosa Luxemburg Stiftung, 2016.

On the one hand, the model proposed by platform cooperativism is aimed at containing the platforms superpower through a complex regulatory intervention, based on the user's privacy protection and the limits over the management of their personal data. On the other hand, it proposes a new solution that redefines the interpretive schemes of the problem. It envisages a new role, the producer:[156] both user and producer. It is a user that owns the platforms he uses and also the contents he produces. As underlined by Trebor Scholz, the model should inspire cases such as the Berlinese Resonate, a cooperative platform dedicated to music streaming. It is owned by its users and used to listen to music or produce music; another case is Stocksy, a marketplace website to sell pictures, owned by a cooperative of photographers. We lack entirely a legislative dimension apt to manage a cooperative approach applied to platforms, probably because the idea of platform cooperativism comes from the US. On the one hand, we are experiencing an extraordinary vitality, with copious ideas and projects about the topic. On the other hand, we deduce these ventures' fragility due to the difficulty of conceiving original solutions to coordinate risks, proprieties, control, and profits, lacking any experimented reference models[157].

Platform capitalism seemed to have definitively moved away from the Net from the ideals of the '90s. According to those ideals, the platforms were third parties, used to guarantee the transactions' righteousness and the connections between the users, like real judges.[158] The platform cooperativism revives those ideals and goes beyond them, linking them to a new platform property model based on the user and his data.

This central position is possible, thanks to two elements:

---

[156] A. Bruns, *Owning Is the New Sharing*, Shareable, 2014.
[157] G. Smorto, *Le regole del Gioco del Platform Cooperativism*,(the rules of the game) Impresa Sociale, 8-2016.
[158] T. Gillespie, *The Politics of Platform*, New Media & Society, May, 2010.

- **The self-sovereign identity[159] concept.** At present, the user's identity in the Web is focused on third platforms' role, managing his data. These platforms have access to the user's information, and they use it to elaborate new information on the user without him being aware. The user, thus, loses control over his data. With a self-sovereign identity model, the user owns his data and decides if, when, and how to share them with third parties;
- **The availability of technologies such as the blockchain** enables approaches based on the self-sovereign identity model. It gives the opportunity not to entrust "a third party" with the integrity of the data connected to one's identity.

If technology allowed the platforms to develop a monopoly position in users' data management, that very same technology offers a solution to contain platforms' role and envisages newly designed ones. Mainly, in this case, Agenda 2030 is a working instrument and a direction to follow. Thanks to technology, we can pursue its goals. But, also, those goals define a horizon to look at for the building of a sustainable society. Platforms will be the main actors in our society, but our job will be to define their role through a series of new rules generated by our choices.

[159] C. Allen, *The Path to Self-Sovereign Identity*, www.lifewithalacrity.com, 25 aprile 2016.

Data society

She could not realize if she was feeling perplexed, guilty, annoyed, or only angry.

At first, she had felt enthusiastic about the offer: one year's work with one of the best teams in the world. In her dream country, moreover. And she was not so young anymore. All thanks to that paper she had worked so hard on.

It would have been like living inside a Grey's Anatomy episode. Or a Dr. House episode. She wouldn't have admitted, but she really enjoyed breaking down all the creative theories, diagnoses, and TV series therapies. However, she really envied all the doctors that had the chance actually to work in those hospitals. Now she was one of them, at least for a while. But for now, eye on the screen, concerned look, and her stethoscope in her hands, risking to break again, that enthusiasm was gone.

It. Was. Right. It. The bloody computer.

Or, to say it better, the artificial intelligence used experimentally for diagnostic support was right. She hadn't paid too much attention to the system's warning while she was entering her data into the Cloud. She had dismissed the warning, shrugging her shoulders. What does a computer know about food disorder? She said to herself. But now, she felt the burden of that mistake on her shoulders. Nothing irreparable, to be true, but she could have saved time and suffering. She was wrong, and she had been warned.

She wasn't sure if the most significant damage was for her patient or her ego. The fact is that tension was fatal to the umpteenth stethoscope.

Carla's diagnosis was wrong. It happens to every doctor every day. What annoys her the most is not the damage to her patient, that luckily is restrained, nor the fact that she was wrong. It happens to everyone. Nor the fact that she had been warned about the mistake. But what hurt her the most was that she had been warned by someone – something – not so different from her microwave hoven. She cannot come to terms with the fact that the artificial intelligence system used in the research center corrected her diagnosis. And it was right about it.

This story depicts the problem between people and digital technologies because they deal with data, information, decisions, choices. Science Fiction and post-apocalyptic movies are the echoes of our fears because people see technology as a threat. A threat for jobs, in the best option. A danger for the future in the worst-case scenario.

However, it is hard for most people in their inner subconscious to distinguish between truth and fantasy, especially when dealing with such emotionally involving issues. To be honest, experts are not in agreement about the possible futures.

From the initial evolution of machines, which started with the industrial revolutions and culminated with big data and quantum information science, our life has really changed and will change more, that is certain.

Data explosion

If one needed to explain with an image what happened over the years about the increase of data produced by computers, the best would probably be an explosion.

A real big bang, considering the magnitude of the event. The link to the big bang is no exaggeration. When we think about information science, we are used to thinking about measurement units such as the *megabyte* or the *gigabyte,*[160] generally used for the storage of pictures, documents, and videos. For smartphones' memory, we use the gigabyte. For computers' storage, we talk about the terabyte.[161]

---

[160] A megabyte corresponds to a million bytes (10^6), while a gigabyte corresponds to a billion bytes (10^9).

[161] A terabyte corresponds to a billion byte (10^{12}), one thousand billion of bytes.

But if we want to reason with the web's data – if any reasoning is possible or even sensible apart from giving us a vague idea – the situation is more complicated.

We need different orders of magnitude to express these numbers, difficult to understand and imagine. Suffice to think about the social network sites. Twitter's users, alone, produce about half a billion tweets every day. WhatsApp's users send about 65 billion messages. And what about the old emails? Apparently, we have about 300 billion of them. Terabytes are not enough to put into numbers the magnitude of data generated daily by Facebook: we need to talk about petabytes,[162] and Zuckerberg's baby produces more than 4 of them. The estimated value of the entire digital universe is about 44.000 exabytes or 44 zettabytes.[163]Nearly 40 times the stars we can observe[164].

If we wanted to print on paper all the new information produced by the Web over a year, the pile would be one billion kilometers high. Like the distance between the Earth and the Moon traveled 1250 times. To and from.

The connection to the astronomical dimension fits perfectly.

These data do not consider the information growth that will be produced by the enhancement of the Internet of things and the diffusion of 5G. By then, it will be necessary to think about other units of measurement.

What are the *big data*?

Nothing is left to the imagination: the prefix refers obviously to an enormous amount of data. As we said, the data volume is measurable with high numbers, but it is not just the quantity that defines the data on the Web. Those data are also very different from one another. On the Internet,

[162] A petabyte corresponds to one thousand billion of bytes (10^{15})
[163] One exabyte corresponds to one billion of billions of bytes (10^{18}), while a zettabyte corresponds to one thousand billion of billions of bytes (10^{21}).
[164] [source: Dataroom, Sole 24Ore, 2019]

we can find any information: social media contents, news, Stock, environmental data gathered from different climate stations all over the world. We can find everything on the Web and in large quantities. Furthermore, some of these data have a limited duration: minutes and even seconds (Stock-exchange information); others can last hours (weather forecasts used to plan a weekend); some others are useful for days or months (the number of inhabitants in a town).

"Volume," "variety,"(meant as the number of types and natures), and "velocity" (both of the transmission and the potential obsolescence of the datum) are the three main features of *big data.*
There are many more; provenance, for example: in the web, the data coming from official sources are mixed up with those produced by the users. Guaranteeing the origin of the firsts and the reliability of the seconds is not simple.

Dealing with data today is more complicated than it used to be in the past for two reasons: the main reason and also the simplest is that the data at our disposal are much more than they were in the past and much more complex to analyze. What is the remedy to complexity? Of course, we need new analysis patterns, helping us deal with the *information overflow* and allowing us to build value over reality so challenging to analyze.

Traditional systems for data analysis are based on the identification of structures employed to explain reality. In other words, we use what we already know to understand and classify what we experience.

It is similar to what Linneo used to do with his classification of the species. When the observed phenomena' complexity grows, the risk that the known structures to describe the unknown are not useful anymore grows simultaneously. The Swedish botanist wouldn't have been happy to meet the platypus, a weird mammal that lays down eggs; it has fur but webbed feet and the beak of a duck. This animal blows up completely Linneo's taxonomy system.[165]The same goes for the other animals discovered in

[165] Binomial nomenclature ("two-term naming system") was published by Linneo in his work Systema Naturae in 1735. The platypus was discovered at the end of that same century.

the following centuries. Linneo structured a classification system based on what he knew. But his knowledge was not enough to describe the material world's complexity because it was based on elementary classification schemes, now replaceable by more complex criteria.

The situation for decision-makers – an individual, a company, or an institution – is not so different from Linneo's. We are used to building schemes to interpret what is around us and to shape our knowledge. These schemes – whether we realize it or not – are innate in our cognitive model.

What happens when the complexity of our surroundings is too high? What happens when the number of information we should be able to cross, understand, classify, and outline is growing exponentially? Then, what happens when the experience of what happened is not useful to understand what will happen in the future? The relation between action and reaction is influenced by unpredictable deductions, impossible to determine with the analysis of what we know.

We talk about the transition from a learning model based on *single-loop learning* (the reaction caused by the action is usually predictable and based on known rules) to *double-loop learning*[166](the reaction caused by the action is affected by inferences that are not predictable). It is the passage from a universe in which we can master the complexities – or at least have the illusion – to a universe in which complexities are so high; we cannot control them using the knowledge we have when we are making our choices[167].

This is the universe of big data. Its starting point is the statistical inference[168] , and the arrival is artificial intelligence.

---

[166] C. Argyris, D.A. Schön, *Organizational Learning: A Theory of Action Perspective*, Addison-Wesley Pub. Co., 1978.

[167] For a detailed study on the subject see, from the same author: S.Epifani Business Community, Costruire capitale Intellettuale nella Net Economy,(Business Community, building Intellectual Capital in the Net Economy), 2003.

[168] Inferential statistics is divided into classic and baynesian statistics. It is the process according to which we deduce a phenomenon's characteristics by the observation of some of its factors. To understand the difference between the inferential statistics and

The analysis techniques based on the big data are used to identify correlations that elude the analyst, but recurring in a given situation can help him understand the event he is analyzing.

For example, in the insurance field, actuarial mathematics is based on tables describing conditions useful to assess the insured's risk. Using the actuarial tables and balancing the financial aspect and probabilities, the insurance agent can evaluate the risk and submit the quote on the customer's potential damages.

Let's take as an example life insurance: it is clear that a lawyer fond of acrobatic skydiving is more in danger than a lawyer with similar features (same age, same salary, same dwelling place) but fond of chess.
Big data analysis works differently. It considers all the possible information coming from all the available sources, whether or not it seems coherent to what we are looking for. It looks, amidst this information, for any significant correlations. Significant means – for example – appeared in other similar contexts, thus defining strong recurring patterns. When assessing the risk of the two lawyers, new unstructured factors will surface. They will confirm that insuring the first lawyer, is not a good idea. They would also show that fond-of-skydiving lawyers who own a Persian cat are less likely to die a horrible death than a bespectacled lawyer fond of gardening.

It is not up to big data analysis to explain to the insurance agent (or the partially-sighted gardner/lawyer) why he is more at risk than his flying cat-lover colleague. It just observes how a determined correlation of facts generates with statistical relevance a specific series of consequences. Without explaining the reasons.

---

the counting principle we make an example: we have an urn, with 6 white balls and 2 red balls. Using the fundamental counting principle it is clear that the probability to extract a red ball is 0.4. But, if we ignore the ratio between the red balls and the white balls and we want to find it out on the base of the color of the extracted balls for a number of times, then we are operating a statistical inference.

Dr. Carla's decision-support system didn't make the diagnosis based on the knowledge of the disease but on the probability deduced from the analysis of different sources, apparently disconnected from the diagnostic goal.

In other terms, big data analysis allows foreseeing what is likely to happen, but not why that thing is happening. It is a matter of "what," not a matter of "why."

It may seem reductive, but this approach is used by the major companies born in the Web age. Companies such as Amazon, Google, Facebook, or Apple base their activities on intercepting users' information and understanding their behaviors, tastes, and preferences. The same goes for all the new infomediaries[169]. The core business of actors such as Booking.com or TripAdvisor is not based on hospitality, food service, or public transport. Booking.com is the owner of no rooms. TripAdvisor's staff could not have set foot in a restaurant. Both of them – and many others – are data companies. They make their money on the ability to value the users' available data and on the ability to offer them, basing on that acquired knowledge, a useful service.

If we talk about actors that base their activity on gathering users' data to infer their behaviors, the problem that arises is not secondary.

It is not so strange to believe that the most potent social media know their users' vote even before the users themselves. They know their intimate relationships without the users being aware. They foresee who we may like, who we may want to meet, who we may fall in love with. And they can act accordingly, supporting the meeting or preventing it.

It is not so risky a theory that the biggest search engines can understand what the user rather sees. They will show the user the contents they prefer, rather than the most important to see, aiming to satisfy their needs

[169] J. Hagel III, *The New Infomediaries*, The McKinsey Quarterly, p. 54 and following, autumn 1997.

and keep them longer on the platform. Or making the user choose that platform over the others.

It is not unlikely to imagine that the combined big data analysis and network analysis could produce a progressive contracture of the events horizon, with which the users connect and their interpretations. Their goal is to make a world shaped on the users, but potentially devoid of objectivity and more and more distant from reality.

It is not a rush to think that data companies use the available information for different scopes. Different from what the users had granted them. Even today, the business model of some online game-producing companies is based on the sale of the behavioral profiles of their users – typically teenagers – to human resources recruitment societies. These societies will use that information to choose or exclude them from some jobs based on their behavior. If you are a *killer*, an *explorer*, or a *socializer*[170] in FortNite,[171] you could be one even when you go to work. The same goes for other apps, tracking the sports activities of runners and sports passionates. The business model is based on the sale of information about the users' state of health. It is deduced by smartphones and smartwatches and then sold to companies, such as insurance corporations.

From *big data* to artificial intelligence

The border between *big data analysis* and artificial intelligence is really thin. Sometimes it is deceptive. If a divide is to be made, it is possible to identify two approaches to the problem of data analysis and creation: one is based on the data, and the other is based on the algorithms[172]. The difference is basically on how the set of rules that determines data management is conceived.

---

[170] Killer, socializer, explorer, achiever are the four game styles identified by Richard Bartle in Hearts, CVlub, Diamonds, Spades: players who suit MUDs, 1996.

[171] FortNite is a multiusers videogame released by Epic Games and People can fly in 2017. In 2019 it registered 250 million of users all over the world.

[172] L. Breiman, *Statistical Modeling: The Two Cultures*, Statistical Science, vol. 16, n. 3, pp. 199-215, Institute of Mathematical Statistics, agosto 2001.

In the first case, we can say that data can vary when dealing with a problem, but the algorithm – regardless of its complexity – is essentially stable. As if we said that the referee could count on the rules' stability no matter the players. This model is conservative, loved by the old statisticians.

In the second case, things get amusing (not for the old statisticians): the algorithm is not necessarily a constant, but in a world getting more and more complex, it can evolve according to the growth of the system it is computing. It is like saying that if the game's conditions change little by little, the rules evolve to manage the change better. In other words: a nightmare for the vintage statisticians.

We need to remember that Big data are born in the first model, but they end up in the second. Even the simple patterns identification referring to the skydiver lawyer and the chess-lover lawyer is based on an algorithm called "machine learning[173]" that – using the so-called artificial neural networks[174] – is an artificial intelligence system. In other terms, when we talk about artificial intelligence, we refer, in general, to those systems based on self-changing algorithms. They change according to what they learn from experience, that is, from the data and the situations they impact.

When we think about artificial intelligence, we cannot help thinking about the reductive and creepy images conveyed by sci-fi authors. The idea that humankind could artificially create intelligence or even build

[173] The term machine learning was coined in 1959 by the engineer Arthur Samuel. His definition was "a field of sudy giving computers the chance to learn without being specifically set up." These are computing systems based on algorithms using the experience to enhance the performances or to make accurate predictions. These algorithm systems are organized as artificial neural networks. (read following note)

[174] The artificial neural networks are postulated for the first time by the neurophysiologists McCulloch and Pitts in 1943. They are computing model made of artificial neurons, inspired to the structure of a biological neural network. The functioning of the artificial neural networks is aimed to reproduce the biological neural networks, made of neurons connected to each other by according to different structures determinating their functionality. These mathematics models are at the basis of artificial intelligence systems.

new knowledge like a demiurge was intriguing at first. Then, it scared hordes of scientists, philosophers, theologists, economists.

This subject concerning the digital field is one of the most fascinating for experts or amateurs, but it is also one of the most misunderstood, mystified, and warped in its essence. For the sole purpose of writing a striking article or laying a claim on the umpteenth – probably useless – bill.

The possible consequences are more devastating if we think that the concept of artificial intelligence is really vast. This same definition, indeed, is used to describe the most various phenomena: from the computers of *"2001: A Space Odyssey*[175]*"* and the Asimovian[176] computers, more human than the humans to the automatic responders of the call centers, irritating the most patient of men.
The first ones – computers and human robots – belong to the category called "strong" artificial intelligence. The one that should reach auto-conscience, and until now, it is confined to sci-fi movies. It is important to clarify: any professionals in their right mind would ever think that an auto-conscious computer would wake up in the morning and, out of the blue, decide to conquer the world. According to Matrix[177], if that should happen, we would notice when it is too late. But according to our present knowledge, the risk is improbable. And even if it is likely, it would be too late to notice: so, why worry?
It is a different story for the automatic responders. They use a "weak" artificial intelligence. It analyses specific issues too complex to be computed by the human brain. That is the case, for example, of the DeepBlue[178] computer that managed to win against the chess World Champion Ivan Kasparov, but that apart from playing chess is entirely useless.

---

[175] 2001: A Space Odyssey is a sci-fi novel written by the British novelist Arthur C. Clarke in 1968. In the same years Stanley Kubrik shot the namesake movie.

[176] Isaac Asimov (1920-1992) was a soviet writer and biologist naturalized American. He wrote several novels and sci-fi stories, some of them have become movies, and also scientific essays

[177] The Matrix is a sci-fi movie written and directed by the Wachowschi brothers in 1999.

[178] Deep Blue was a computer released by IBM, designed to play chess. It was the first calculator to win a chess match against the World Champion, Garry Kasparov, on the 10th of February 1996. However Kasparov won the 3 of the following matches and tied 2.

Strong artificial intelligence, for now, is confined to sci-fi movies; as for weak artificial intelligence, we will come upon it in the years to come, and maybe – without noticing – we already have.

The applications are infinite:

- It is used to suggest the best products according to the user's behavior and his previous purchases by the e-commerce systems;
- It is used by urban security to analyze the CCTV footage in towns or places of public interest, to identify potentially dangerous situations to support law enforcement;
- It is used in domestic automation and gives voice (and capacity) to the vocal assistants that now are hosted in houses;
- It is used to prevent potential frauds by analyzing the habits of users, and any exceptions, probably connected to fraudulent activities;
- It is used for videogames to make the characters more realistic;

The list could go on. Concerning this list, most people would consider artificial intelligence to be an opportunity. Still, many others would see it as a threat because it replaces men in repetitive jobs and intellectual activities.

For example, we do not need strong artificial intelligence to write a newspaper article. It is not the declaration of Valerio's dystopia, in which an artificial intelligence system replaces him. Today, realities such as the Associated Press and the Washington Post use this instrument to produce some particular news automatically. Artificial intelligence will create in a few seconds – from more or less structured data to sophisticated language processing systems – hundreds of articles. For now, its applications are related to simple semantic structures, like sportscast, or financial articles, weather forecast. These topics are based on glossaries using recurring statements that can be easily arranged. Seconds before closing the Exchange, it is possible to assemble an article for each quoted factory. Or at the end of matches, an article about every game. It is evident; this will affect the journalists' jobs. It is important to underline how this change could go two different directions: we can focus on the negative effects, highlighting the possible decrease in employment for journalists, replaced by machines. Or we can focus on the positive aspects, highlighting how this application could provide more resources. It could also grant free time to do activities and actions we do not have time for. Probably, both answers are realistic. The right solution will depend on how the sector will act: it could choose a profit-oriented logic over the quality of the information. Or it could choose to offer a better service to the readers, in an economic sustainability context, generated by the integration of human intelligence and artificial instruments.

Once again, we need to decide whether to choose a Red Flag Act or to face innovation and seize the opportunities, rather than hide behind a defense line to avoid – in vain – the risks.

The same will happen for highly qualified professions. We saw it with Carla, the doctor who made a mistake. It does not mean that being a doctor is obsolete. The supporting-decision systems used for diagnosis do not replace the doctors: on the contrary, they implement their job and make it more efficient. They enable doctors to make more accurate diagnoses using a computing capacity that no doctor could ever have. Artificial intelligence gleans knowledge from the vast archives and can learn from thousands of doctors' experience, implementing its algorithms to make more accurate suggestions. Every doctor can take advantage of this significant capacity. The same goes for other jobs: from lawyers to architects, from physicists to computer scientists.

Far from auto-conscious computers and Matrix scenarios, weak artificial intelligence, weak only by name, will produce stronger and stronger impacts on the economy, market, and society.

We need to bear in mind that wicked, matrix-style computers will not cause our future issues. In fact, the rules set on the unaware computers will be determined by humans.

Risks are just behind the corner. The *machine learning* algorithms for decision-making are based on the analysis of structured information. What would happen, then, if the structured information we give them is warped? What would happen if thousands of human selectors entrust an "educated" artificial intelligence with the sorting of human resources? The artificial intelligence would "learn" all the humans' prejudices, which would become an essential part of its decisional and behavioral scheme. With the results of preferring white men over black men or men over women. It has already happened. The risk of developing a cognitive bias[179] in artificial intelligence is real. The consequence will be to create a system that will inherit the prejudices far from being more fair and reliable than humans. In defiance of several of Agenda 2030's points. Such as **Goal 8**: *Promote sustained, inclusive and sustainable economic growth, full and productive employment, and decent work for all.* Just to name those connected to the recruiting.

The real challenge is to understand the importance of those who write the algorithms for future computers and how these algorithms will be written. We need to know how these algorithms will be "educated" and what kind of data they will use because a consistent part of our lives will be regulated on the basis of these algorithms.

That is why it is essential to broaden the conception of data openness. On its base, public interest data should be freely accessible by the algorithms: we talk about open data, and also open algorithms, or transparent algorithms. It is fundamental for the building of sustainable development that the public interest algorithms – no matter if coming from public structures, institutions, or privates - be transparent. This is the only way to develop a sustainable and open society in which artificial intelligence is at humankind's service.

Big data and artificial intelligence for sustainability

When dealing with technology, people tend to focus on possible issues more than the possibilities they disclose. Particularly when dealing with technologies such as big data or artificial intelligence. The thoughts run fast towards the sci-fi catastrophic scenarios. Even the landmark figures for the development of information science that changed – with their

---

[179] C. Radfar, *Bias In AI: A problem recognized but still unresolved*, TechCrunch, 2019.

ideas – our society's face show their conservative side about artificial intelligence. Bill Gates declared more than once his will to levy taxes on those factories that prefer artificial intelligence over human labor. As if we should tax the launderettes for using washing machines instead of washerwomen. These stances are sometimes due to the emotional surge upsetting society and also to the need for visibility. Anycase, to be true to history, these positions are to blame. They risk emphasizing the contrast between human and artificial intelligence. The discrepancy is due to the choice of wording – artificial intelligence – that evokes more fear than enthusiasm.

Let's look beyond the contrasts (mostly about terminology) and start experiencing these technologies for what they are (or should be): instruments at our service; then we understand the importance of managing them properly. Because if misused, they can produce severe damage, but they can be powerful allied for sustainable development with correct use.

It is the case of the Child Growth Monitor project, created by the German ONG Welthungerhilfe together with Microsoft, to hinder Indian children's malnutrition. The project is inspired by **Goal 2:** *End hunger, achieve food security, and improved nutrition, and promote sustainable agriculture.* The goal is to detect malnutrition and health standards by analyzing some basic parameters such as height, body mass, and the ratio between weight and wrist circumference. The system is based on a smartphone app that – resorting to artificial intelligence – files analyzes, and elaborates the data to give directions to the final users, supporting local communities to handle malnutrition. This app has been developed experimentally to monitor malnutrition phenomena in the most impoverished areas of the world. Still, the operating principle for its use in the wealthiest areas is the same. So if we decided to use it in the developed countries to control overnutrition, then we would match correctly **Goal 3:** *Ensure healthy lives and promote well-being for all at all ages.* According to Unicef, the situation in Italy is as follows: the children and teenagers obesity rate in Italy is 36%. Numbers do not lie: from 2000 to 2016, the percentage of overweight children from 5 to 19 years old doubled, from 1 out of 10 to 1 out of 5. Moreover, in relation to 1990, it grew by about 39,1%[180]. These data profoundly affect children's health. We need to take action to create a proper food culture. We could use these systems flanked by gamification systems to foster the use and apps to guarantee the spread on a large scale. It would be crucial for the building of sensible society. It is essential to underline that the apps used in extreme conditions frameworks can also be used in totally different contexts.

Artificial intelligence would prove efficient in another important milieu: the management of public resources. Especially if the resources are scarce. It is the situation in many areas of the world concerning water management. Agenda 2030 focused one of its goals entirely on this delicate issue. **Goal 6**: *Ensure availability and sustainable management of water and sanitation for all.* Access to water is a fundamental right, but often its availability and management make the problem difficult to solve. To cope with the issue, Melbourne Water, in Australia, uses a specifically designed platform. This platform controls the pumps' movement inside the water pipes according to the quantity of water used on a particular day. This action will empower predictive algorithms that, based on experience, will estimate the usage for the following days[181]. Artificial intelligence, thus, allows the reduction of waste and enhances the systems' functioning, with considerable economic saving and a lesser environmental impact.

Thinking about another significant urban infrastructure, moving from sustainable water management to transportation, we need to read **Goal 11**: *Make cities and human settlements inclusive, safe, resilient and sustainable.* In this sense, London's case is particularly significant[182]. In London,

---

[180] The State of the World's Children, Unicef, 2019 *Children, food and nutrition: Growing well in a changing world*

[181] Read **Target 6.4**: By 2030, substantially increase water-use efficiency across all sectors and ensure sustainable withdrawals and supply of freshwater to address water scarcity and substantially reduce the number of people suffering from water scarcity

[182] We refer to:

- **Target 11.2**: By 2030, provide access to safe, affordable, accessible and sustainable transport systems for all, improving road safety, notably by expanding public transport, with special attention to the needs of those in vulnerable situations, women, children, persons with disabilities and older persons

thanks to the big data on transportation and the users' data, they are working on the enhancement of pedestrians' services and transportation interchanges included subway and railway services. The goal is to create real-time routes for the users, thanks to the interchange between different means of transport. This action aims to reduce the impact on car traffic and make the streets safer and suitable for leisure walks. This project is included in London Municipality's bigger frame, using systematically the technologies based on big data and artificial intelligence from 2015. Sao Paulo's Municipality, in Brazil, is on the same page. It is gathering all data from the telephone network as well, from 2018. In cooperation with Vivo (a Telefònica Brazil brand mobile), the Municipality collects the data produced by the users' smartphones. Then, it deduces the live-traffic situation, the busiest urban routes, and infers the pollution levels. These data are used - in real-time – to reshape at best the transportation routes and the public services, to help to fight pollution and smog in the Brazilian town[183].

Big data and artificial intelligence are the instruments for developing smart cities, sustainable and inclusive, and dealing with illegal fishing as underlined in Target 4 of Goal 14: Conserve and sustainably use the oceans, seas, *and marine resources for sustainable development*. An attractive solution is proposed by an Italian reality, the startup Studiomapp. The company developed a system using artificial intelligence to analyze the oceans' satellite imagery to identify the number of boats, their position, the fishing activities, the deliveries, and all the marine side activities worldwide. Everything is possible thanks to the artificial intelligence able to cross and understand the satellite imagery and confront it with AIS[184] data. The system can track and signal the boats perpetrating illegal fishing or in protected areas.

- **Target 11.7:** By 2030, provide universal access to safe, inclusive and accessible, green and public spaces, in particular for women and children, older persons and persons with disabilities

[183] In particular read **Target 11.6:** By 2030, reduce the adverse per capita environmental impact of cities, including by paying special attention to air quality and municipal and other waste management

[184] Automatic Identification System, a compulsory subsidiary system used by ships and vessel traffic services, mainly for their identification and position.

From the sea to the woods: in California, the authorities started to use big data and artificial intelligence to prevent the fires in woods next to the urban and rural areas, determining the development trend in advance. The WiFIRE system puts together historical records on the fires and real-time measurements from aero-photogrammetry to satellite imagery, from the weather stations to other sensors of the Internet of Things. Similar systems also developed in Great Britain and Greece. These initiatives match **Goal 15**: *Protect, restore, and promote sustainable use of terrestrial ecosystems, sustainably manage forests, combat desertification, and halt and reverse land degradation and halt biodiversity loss.*

When dealing with big data and artificial intelligence, it is vital to think about sustainability to support their development as economic and social well-being instruments. **Goal 8**: *Promote sustained, inclusive, and sustainable economic growth, full and productive employment, and decent work for all,* which must be our beacon. People who see technological development as a problem more than an opportunity focus their attention on the potential impacts of technologies on the labor world and economy. That is why we need to ask the right questions on the matter of technologies.

As it happened before with the loom or the production line, artificial intelligence has the power to destroy millions of jobs. That is why we do not need to ask whether technology will have good or bad impacts on society, but how to make those impacts positive. Concretely it means to take advantage of the opportunities to produce sustainable, decent, inclusive work. We need to act promptly to seize them. We need to bear in mind the targets of Goal 8 and build effective strategies starting from them, using artificial intelligence to put them to action. Too often, we talk about ethics technology or – in particular – artificial intelligence ethics. But we tend to forget that ethics is not about technologies; it is about how people decide to enhance them. It is not the time yet for auto-conscious computers and new moral and ethical models. Still, we need to remember that the development of economic models based on weak artificial intelligence must be oriented towards sustainable development promoted by Agenda 2030.

The lie of disintermediation

The internet was born as a distributed network. Its development was fostered by its distributed and decentralized approach. Together with PCs spread, it contributed to establishing our model of computer science. However, the development of the cloud and the platforms challenged this model, which is facing a process of re-centralization.

The SaaS model enabled by *cloud computing* – that is to say, the possibility to distribute the software functions as if they were services accessible through the Web rather than installing them on the PC – has two possible interpretations. On the one hand, it facilitates the spread of the applications for users who otherwise would not have the knowledge and the competence to use them. The advantage *of cloud computing,* in this sense, is visible. The simplification enabled by *cloud computing* makes the spread of applications easier, supports the standardization of the processes, favors the users with scarce competencies and low budgets. In short, it is a real development booster. On the other hand, the extensive use of *cloud* systems engenders serious issues. It produces a strong centralization towards a limited number of operators, *the cloud providers,* and the platforms, not only providing software solutions but also keeping the users' data and the operative processes.
These operators have a central role that will increase in the future. They can create strong *lock-in* mechanisms able to influence the activities of the client companies decisively. Moreover, thinking about the platforms' role, they handle billions of users'data, becoming key junctions in a Web less and less de-centered, shaping like a few-pointed star.

In short, we moved from the disintermediation web to the web of the new intermediaries. They have high power, growing more and more.

We still believe in the misunderstanding that the Net produced a disintermediation process. Actually, it started a great re-intermediation process, in which new operators replaced, and will replace the old ones.

Often we confuse this process with the *sharing economy,* but the sharing economy has nothing to do with these phenomena:

- Uber did not disintermediate radio taxis: it is a radio taxi in an App.
- AirBnB and Booking.com did not disintermediate the travel agencies: they are travel agencies without an office, they reach the users through the smartphone.
- eBay and Amazon did not disintermediate the shops; they are shops.

Using the push from social media development and the possibilities offered by big data and artificial intelligence, these actors create value from the users and supply services behaving like intermediaries. Rather, like "infomediaries," according to John Hagel III's definition from his historical essay, The New Infomediaries, 20 years old but still up-to-date.

Nothing strange. However, it is clear that these new infomediaries have a great responsibility. And it is clear that their activity is – and will be – more and more critical, not only for the economic dimension of the action but also for social sustainability. Because their activity is connected to actors that possess great information capital about the users. This capital, never in human history, was concentrated in the hands of such few factories. It is then clear the necessity to reshape the international regulations that establish their existence to define how and where their power ends. Their national power is void, everyone agrees, except those who consider the Web as an instrument for easy visibility, when it happens to be the only option, but this is another story. Everything in order. These operators respect the rules given by different countries. These rules were conceived for an analogic world, and sometimes they find it challenging to adapt to the dynamism and fastness of the digital dimension. These rules need reshaping, sooner or later. That is why we need alternatives.

Blockchain between disintermediation and (mis)trust

As thing stands, thinking about possible alternatives to the superpower of the platforms, the most interesting option could be the *blockchain*.

We need the conditional clause because, with blockchain, we are experiencing experiments, hypotheses, bets, lucubration like never before, without producing functioning cases of usage. Today the only successful case of blockchain is bitcoin, thanks to which the blockchain is famous. Bitcoin is the first and most important cryptocurrency. It is concerning the financial world and offering unexpected and sometimes fleeting wealth, with the risk of losing people a lot of money, but also making people dream a bit. Cryptocurrency or virtual coins are digital vectors designed to work as a medium of exchange using cryptography to secure economic compensation. They do not have any legal tender in most parts of the world. They are not ruled by any governance institutions or central banks. They are – only – virtual bonds (in the strict sense), whose value is established by the users' acceptance. Like objects to barter. That is why, together with their digital dimension (an object has an intrinsic value, a *bitcoin token*[185] does not), their market value is extremely volatile. Bitcoins' success is connected mainly to their incredible quotation growth over the years[186]. This growth shook the foundations of the financial world that is trying to understand – with some effort – how to cope with virtual currencies.

Bitcoins and their epigones are literally revolutionizing the Finance world, and yet, cryptocurrency is just one of the possible applications of the blockchain.

What is then the blockchain? Why is it boding to be one of the most important innovations of the last years?

The blockchain is a "Distributed Ledger Technology" (DLT), a technology that is based on a distributed ledger.

DLT systems allow, thanks to the Web technology, to rethink in a new and interesting way, the processes that involve the recording of transactions between two parties efficiently and safely. Such as the sale of a house, the subscription of a contract, study certifications, the exchange of virtual and physical goods, or for bitcoins, currency (even if virtual).

---

[185] A token is an abstraction of value linked to an object – real or virtual – to which an exchange unit is related. A chip in a casino is a token, a meal voucher is a token. Or a bitcoin.

[186] Referring to the last 5 years the value of the bitcoin increased of 2.500%.

For hundreds of years, we have been recording contracts and transactions in what has been called many names, but fundamentally is the dear old ledger: a public register used to transcribe contracts. The transcription of the contract (or, in general, any transaction) in the register confirms its validity. Obviously, to verify its legal effect, the management rests on a Superior Institution: the Notary, the Municipality, the Certification Authority. (please, the reader use the Capital Intonation To Give Authority To The Overmentioned Actors.)

What would happen if technology allows people to have an updated copy at their disposal, with all the validated transactions, secure, transparent, unmodifiable, classified? What if, potentially, will it eliminate the mediation of a Superior Institution? This would mean a real revolution, from the certification bodies and public registers' role to the traditional intermediation models (from the marketplace to the stock exchange.)

This is possible thanks to the DLT, of which the blockchain is the commonest. The distributed ledger enabled by these technologies allows this action: there is no need to go to the notary to register a deed; the registration becomes valid when everyone has the deed in their archives, which are called – in the case of bitcoins – wallets.

This does not mean that notaries or certification bodies are useless. Their role is modified. Because – and this fact needs clarifying – the blockchain can guarantee the validity of the transaction (the exchange from A to B), but it cannot guarantee the quality of the content. For example, the use of blockchain for quality monitoring in the food industry, in particular, the wine sector. It can confirm that the operator Tom poured something he called Chianti into a bottle and gave that bottle to Dick. The blockchain does not have – and never will – the ability to go into the transaction details and will never have the power to change cheap wine into Barolo.

The blockchain can guarantee a transaction not to be modified once agreed upon and verified by a coherent number of actors. Every time exchange is made, it needs to be validated by all the actors to be effective. They receive a notice of the trade and confirm the validity consequently.

So, every wallet of every bitcoins owner possesses – anonymously – every bitcoin transaction from the origin. It is clear then that whenever a transaction (called a block) is made, it joins the others (forming a chain: here comes the name blockchain). With the present technological knowledge, it is impossible to modify because we should be able to handle all the wallets of all the bitcoins owners simultaneously.

Two factors are obvious:

- The more users participate, the safer is the blockchain. That is to say, a DLT made with few blocks is as (un)safe as any other database;
- Blockchain technology does not use the software and hardware sources efficiently. A system that replicates a database on every user's computer is not so good at managing the band and the connected resources. In other words, if we are working on applications that require real-time elaboration or carried out in critical situations of band and filing resources, then the blockchain is not the right solution. Not to mention the energy consumption to generate bitcoins and manage the transactions. To give an idea: if bitcoins were a country, it would be the fortieth country in the world for energy consumption, between Austria and Cile. Not an example of sustainability.

Nonetheless, the change of scheme enabled by the DLT has a significant impact: these technologies could represent for transactions what the internet represented for data. In this sense, the blockchain solves a thorny problem about the Web (and not only): the trust amongst stranger actors. Some refer to it as the trust technology, but maybe it should be better to call it the (mis)trust technology. Actually, this is the strong point: it develops a dynamic according to which all the actors involved in the transaction do not need to trust each other. Technology itself makes it impossible (or at least reasonably difficult) to tamper with the process allowing people to trust – if not one another – the technology.

The technological complexity is really high, and the functioning model requires a high data redundancy. Still, the applications can be various: from cryptocurrency – the killer application thanks to which we got to know the blockchain – to a more concrete sharing economy, in which sharing does not request the presence of intermediaries to manage the users' information. It is a Social network without a central platform, in which everyone owns their data, according to the model of the self-sovereign identity, but also smart contracts that do not need the presence of a third party, clauses activating accordingly to different conditions (that need to be verified); management processes for industries controlled and validated by the "community" of the actors; also credit management systems in which every subscriber has been granted his rights by a platform made by all the other subscribers.

With the blockchain, the platform is the users' total: a platform that, void of any central dimension and any value extraction mechanism, can be a real alternative to the actual models.

Blockchain for sustainability

Even if blockchain usage – due to its young age in contexts different from the cryptocurrency – is not so widespread, there are many possible application fields for this technology, from social economics to sustainability.

One of the most debated is the management of the election process through blockchain-based systems. Potentially the blockchain is a powerful, inclusive instrument for citizens in the definition of public policies and participation in the democratic processes, as underlined by **Goal 11**: *Make cities and human settlements inclusive, safe, resilient and sustainable*. However, it is important to highlight the doubts raised by eminent sources. In particular, the problem is not about the management of the election process but – generally speaking – the electronic vote's reliability, considering the current technological ecosystem[187].
According to ENISA[188] , at present, we cannot guarantee the complete security of the voting process related to the analogic vote, with the

[187] *Election cybersecurity: challenges and opportunities*, ENISA, 2019.
[188] ENISA is the European Union Agency for Cybersecurity, born in 2004

election ballot in the ballot box. There is something one cannot digitalize. And even if blockchain could be the right solution for the management of a section, it is not enough to guarantee the whole process in its complexity. As we said, the technological ecosystem's role is central, even related to using a specific technology.

We are not in the electronic elections age yet, but we should be in the digital identity age certified through the blockchain. Blockchain permits the digital identification of people unequivocally, with an approach based on the self-sovereign identity. The information – once certificated – stays in the citizen's hands and is not shared with other actors (within certain limits, not even with public actors), and it appears particularly appropriate for identity certification of the citizens living in risk areas. Think about the Colombian *desplazados*[189], hiding from the RAFC[190] reprisals or the right-wing paramilitary forces. They, of course, tend to keep their identity and whereabouts secret. Certifying the identity with blockchain - so that there would not be any register – allows them to use the services with ID access, such as basic financial services or money transfer. The relation to **Goal 1:** *End poverty in all its forms everywhere*[191] is clear, but there are many more application fields.
A methodological approach based on the *self-sovereign identity* can be implemented in other situations apart from the critical Colombian one. For example, the Estonian government implements the blockchain to certificate a great number of transactions between the government and the citizens, from justice services to health services following **Goal 16:** *Promote peaceful and inclusive societies for sustainable development, provide access to justice for all and build effective, accountable and inclusive institutions at all levels*[192].

---

[189] In Spanish dispersed

[190] revolutionary armed forces of colombia (RAFC)

[191] In detail **Target 1.4** *By 2030, ensure that all men and women, in particular the poor and the vulnerable, have equal rights to economic resources, as well as access to basic services, ownership and control over land and other forms of property, inheritance, natural resources, appropriate new technology and financial services, including microfinance*

[192] In particular:

Another context making technological experimentation about blockchain and in general DLT is the one related to **Goal 12:** *Ensure sustainable consumption and production patterns*[193] and **Goal 13:** *Take urgent action to combat climate change and its impacts*[194], for example, related to the applications for the management of energy efficiency certifications, such as the white certificate[195].
The white certificates can be traded and valorized on the market platform managed by GME[196] or through bilateral negotiation. All the actors joining the mechanism are registered in the Electronic Register of Energy Efficiency Certificates managed by the GME, and the value of the obligations is determined during the exchange sessions in the market[197]. Blockchain – thanks to its characteristics – can be an ideal token of exchange in these situations, allowing the creation of an energy blockchain, in which all the owners of "tokenized" white certificates can exchange them without the intervention of a central actor.

Shifting from energy savings and climate change to pollution, we are dealing with **Goal 14:** *Conserve and sustainably use the oceans, seas, and marine resources for sustainable development.* Fascinating experimentation is that of ONG Plastic Bank. It released with IBM support a certification system for plastics collecting and recycling industries in the developing countries to avoid the scattering in the oceans. To prevent the disposal at sea, every user has been given a token corresponding to a sum, and– according to the plastic he

- Target 16.6: *Develop effective, accountable and transparent institutions at all levels*
- Target 16.7: *Ensure responsive, inclusive, participatory and representative decision-making at all levels*

[193] Target 12.2 *By 2030, achieve the sustainable management and efficient use of natural resources*

[194] Target 13.2: *Integrate climate change measures into national policies, strategies and planning*

[195] the white certificates are tradable obligations to certificate a certain target of energy saving. It requires to undertake energy efficiency measures

[196] Gestore dei Mercati Energetici (Italian Power Exchange) is the exchange for electricity trading in Italy.

[197] Source: GME.

brings to the waste disposal plant – he can spend that money. In this case, Blockchain guarantees the transparency and righteousness of the process, which would be hard to track if using cash or other prizes, and it would be hard to avoid mischievous business.

Blockchain, as we said, is an entirely new technology in its applications other than cryptocurrency. We still need to understand what the most useful setting will be. It is certain, though, - as for any disruptive technology – that the major complexity is to foresee the possible developments basing on the present situation of context, considering that its nature tends to change the contexts.
That is why we need to understand the dynamics to identify the levers to create sustainable development models. The theories on distributed social network sites and sharing economy models used to disintermediate the platforms will be achievable only if we will be able to determine the right direction for this technology and what it will be in the future.

What do things become?

Domenico didn't like chaos. That's why mornings and nights were his favorite times of the day. Early mornings, when no one was around yet. Late nights, when there was no one left. The rest of the day was only a long annoying interlude of pains in the neck. Not that he didn't like people, but he preferred his plants.

Especially now that he wasn't compelled to go around the nursery a thousand times to check on the greenhouses. Now, if he entered a greenhouse, it was because he intended to. How wonderful! It is like visiting a relative because you have to or going freely because you really want to.

In fact, he didn't have to keep an eye on the plants like he used to. The temperature in greenhouses was always supervised, the same for humidity and many other chemical-physical parameters. Thanks to the sensors positioned everywhere, he could manage the situation majestically, and the management system intervened automatically to balance the main factors.

Passing through the barn, he cast a glance over the old seeder—all the time spent to fill the plateaus. Now, thanks to the new intelligent seeders, that activity was wholly automatized. People used to make fun of him and his obsession with technology. That's because they didn't have to wake at four in the morning to seed.

And yet, he couldn't get rid of the old seeder. In the beginning – he told himself – because he could always go back to it. Now he knew he was fond of that tool, a bit rusty, but it reminded him of where it had started. Where he was going was yet to tell, day by day.

Digital technology really changed Domenico's life. Scattered sensors control the physical-chemical parameters allowing him to intervene precisely on the causes of potential pathologies in a targeted way. More physics (controlled irrigation to drop the risk of rotting, monitored humidity to avoid mold, chemical-physical soil analysis for the integration of minerals), and fewer chemicals (such as fertilizers and herbicides) in what is called precision farming or *smart farming*.

This solution makes farming sustainable and healthy, without drifting in models such as the biodynamics that, as efficient as it is, it would require too vast fields to guarantee economic sustainability for the farming factories, even the most motivated. Not to mention the esoteric horn-manure, often connected to these models.

In many layers of the population, these models conveyed the idea that healthy farming means a real getaway from technology. As if it should be impossible to use technology to make farming healthier. The idea of "being better off when things were worst" goes beyond agriculture and embraces many other sectors in Italy. Here, the concept of tradition contrasts with innovation, preventing factories from adding value to tradition through innovation. The instruments of innovation will have a more and more pervasive presence in our society and economy.

The *internet* of things: when things start thinking

The spread of the Web and social network sites contributed (even too much) to tearing down the wall of mistrust towards the digital dimension of reality. Cloud computing extended the impact of digital instruments to the realities void of any technological knowledge. Big data and artificial intelligence made software and applications resilient and flexible. The cost of electronic components dropped significantly over the last few years. The 5G standard connects in high speed and low latency every object on the Web. We are stepping into the Internet of Things Age.

Everything is going to change.

Everything will change because giving a connection to every device will not only make it a connected one. The smartphone is not merely a telephone connected to the internet, a smartwatch is not just an online watch, smart cars are not only cars with web access, and smart objects will not be simply connected. In the internet of things age, connecting an object to the web means, for better or worse, to give it an information logic. It means changing the interaction scheme between the object itself

and the reality reached through that same object. Transforming Domenico's greenhouses into smart greenhouses makes them connected to the web and also changes how they work, time management, and business models. And this goes for every object in our lives. Over the last few years, we witnessed the spread of virtual assistants such as Google Home or Alexa in our houses. These devices enter our homes disguised as advanced radios. Still, thanks to their ability to connect, through simple interfaces, to the objects in a house, making it a smart home, they reshape the interactions with the house itself entirely. They affect the design, the balance of the space, the movements, the interaction patterns with the house services, and, eventually, the user's life and habits.
It is way too simplistic and reductive to look at the internet of things with a sarcastic smile, thinking that connecting a microwave oven to the internet is useless. It was the same with those who reckoned that telephones in a house were unnecessary, that mobiles were just for few people, and social media would not have spread. These objects intercepted a series of dormant needs and helped to satisfy them. They contributed profoundly to change people's social behaviors and habits. It is a tremendous methodological mistake trying to classify the future through the schemes of our present, even more, because technologies overturn these schemes. Prominent personalities used to make this very same mistake: Charlie Chaplin[198] stated that the public was not interested in the audio for cinema; in 1932, Albert Einstein[199] declared that producing atomic energy was not possible; Robert Metcalfe[200] – to talk about technologies –

---

198 When, late in the '20s the spoken was introduced in the cinema, Charlie Chaplin made a stand against it, because he considered it to be a regression towards the teather. He wrote to the Times saying that "miming only is the base of drama." He changed his mind, inserting music, sonorous effects and brief dialogues in the movies *City lights* (1931) and Modern Times (1936). In the end, he reached celebrity with one of the most iconic scene in the world of cinema: the final monologue of the film The Great Dictator (1940). [source: Charlie Chaplin's Talking Pictures, The New Yorker Magazine.]

199 In 1932, after the discovery of the neutron, he declared "we have no certainty that energy will be attainable. It would implicate the atom to be utterly disintegrated"(The New York Times Archive, 2nd of February 1964)

200 Robert Metcalfe was a pioneer of the Web, invetor of the Ethernet network, and founder of the 3Com. In 1995, in the article for the magazine Infoworld the stated: Internet 'will soon go spectacularly supernova and in 1996 will collapse.'(infoworld.com)

invented the Ethernet[201] protocol and preconized the internet collapse within the same year. Predictions on the future made looking at the past or – at the most – at the present moment do not work so well anymore.

The IoT will be for objects what social networks were for relations: social network sites tore down the wall between real and virtual related to relations, keeping the difference between online and offline, at the most. Similarly, the Internet of things demolishes the barrier between analogic and digital, material, and immaterial, giving every object the features of a digital device.

With the internet of things, every object will potentially:

- Have a name (and an IP[202] address) to be identified on the web;
- Be connected and thus reachable through the internet;
- Be given sensors to supply information regarding the surroundings;
- Making more or less complicated functions, autonomously, semi-autonomously, or controlled by remote.

These four combined characteristics will enable every smart object to be a real information device, with all the implications. For better or for worse.

For better, because the IoT allows the development of new services and new applications that make people's lives easier and comfortable and enable new solutions that were inconceivable before. The connection to the Web makes these objects flexible, adaptable to the context and the user's needs, and able to reshape their features according to the users' needs. The sensors allow these objects to detect information on the environment and give it back to the users and other objects. This leads to creating service models based on the building of complex digital ecosystems in

---

[201] The ethernet network is a series of standard technologies for the creation of local networks. They were invented by Robert Metcalfe and David Boggs, and commercialized between 1980 and 1983. There are three types: local network (LAN), metropolitan area network (MAN) and wide area network (WAN). [source: Encyclopaedia Britannica]

[202] The IP address is, in the TCP/IP protocol, the univocal numerical label assigned to each computer or any other device connected to the network.

which the different devices share data and information with one another and with us.

In the worst, because with IoT, the connected devices will talk about us, with other objects, and with us. This will be a great advantage for the users, but it also poses complex issues requiring immediate intervention. For example, privacy issues. Data protection is more and more challenging to achieve. In our context, the private sphere boundary is more and more eroded by the sharing wave of social network sites. Also, by the presence in our homes, workplaces, and lives of all the devices designed to acquire and manage all the users' information, given willingly or not.
And more, when the computer logics enter the objects, they bring all the potential of information science and its problems: first of all, security. A smart car is not just an object connected to the internet to do the upgrade, being connected to the web, but it faces all the possible risks, like any other computer. The difference is that if a hacker entered a user's PC, he could delete, at the most, some pictures of a holiday or maybe some unnecessary paperwork, not saved in a backup. But what if the same hacker entered the self-driving system of a car and sabotaged the brake? We do not need to mention other applications: from pacemakers to air traffic control or a town electric energy.
It is true that IoT tears down the barrier between virtual and real, but it is also true that together with opportunities, it brings in the real world all the issues of the digital.

Today, it is difficult to envisage the future dynamics of a world that by 2030 will have more than 125 billion devices connected to the net[203]. More than 15 devices per person, counting newborns, centenarians, and people living in the far corners of the world.

Today we find ourselves in the condition to lay the foundations of a new society. It will be a society in which humankind could be either the center of a web it can rule or be ruled. This will depend on the choices we will make in the next years.

---

[203] Source: IHS Markit

The *internet* of things for sustainability

The rapid IoT development brings to our attention the necessity to find a solution for the management of the processes and phenomena generated by the presence of digital logic. It is also true that this logic, in its functional perspective, enables new operating paradigms in every sector.
Think about the possibility of telehealth. The connected devices are everyday objects such as microwave ovens or bicycles, but also medical devices for telemonitoring or telediagnosis and vital devices such as the pacemaker. In a society getting older and older, it is fundamental to monitor the expenditure in the health sector to provide a better service (and for a service tout court). Technology, in this field, is literally essential. We refer to **Goal 3:** *Ensure healthy lives and promote well-being for all at all ages*. The availability of connected medical devices allows managing a brand new way through the healing phase and prevention, screening, and monitoring. The very same smartphone becomes a medical device. The Italian project BlueHeart, for example, allows linking, through Bluetooth, a particular electrocardiograph to the smartphone. It enables low-cost screening and telecardiology services 24/7, even in the remotest area of the world. Reached by a connection, of course. Not to mention the smartwatches: they have powerful functions, such as sensors to monitor vital functions like heart rate and blood oxygen levels, to be considered real medical devices. These devices' power and flexibility could be the most significant problem IoT brings about if the users do not develop their knowledge. Jogging with an electrocardiograph recording the strain during the sports performance is a positive thing. It is a positive thing that he wants to share his achievements with his friends. Competition is a motivation to do better. The negative aspect is that our runner, whether informed or not, allowed the app's manager to access his data about his time and his routes. Even worse, if he decided to accept a consent form with carelessness, giving the manager of the app full power to access the registered data and maybe use them for commercial purposes (anyway, who reads the consent forms when downloading apps on their mobiles?) Now, the smartwatch could register an arrhythmia, even before the runner himself would notice. What if the app's owners sold the data to a health insurance company interested in evaluating heart attack risks before submitting life insurance? Or to a head hunter interested in hiring

for a key job? In a world of connected objects, the problem of awareness about the dynamics of data management would become serious. We do not need a conditional clause because we already live in a world of connected objects. That is why every person needs to be aware of the risks and opportunities disclosed by these scenarios.
IoT also means a great contribution to the achievement of **Goal 7:** *Ensure access to affordable, reliable, sustainable, and modern energy for all.* IoT is one of the enabling element for the development of *smart grid* systems. Thanks to which the electrical systems are managed as computer networks. Thanks to the sensors, energy itself becomes smart, in the broad sense, producing a real change in the energy distribution. Treating electric wires as computer networks allows optimizing the electrical load, minimizing the breakdowns, dropping the costs, and making the distribution more flexible. Also, the decentralization of the energy production sites will allow access in the energy market to the small-and-medium-sized producers, that following the internet pattern, could supply energy even if they are not the wires' owners. Just like you do not need a cable to connect the PC with a server, every user can reach any operator in a smart grid system. And vice versa. And every user can become – thanks to a distributed generation approach – both dealer and producer. It is a system that, like the Internet, is a network of interconnected networks to optimize the electrical energy distribution, enhancing the service. This service acquires all the potential of computer services, and also all the possible vulnerabilities. An IoT system is nothing more than a computer system extended to physical objects. What would happen if a hacker attacked that system? Most of a town's vital functions depend on electrical energy distribution, so the potential risk is severe. Operating rooms, traffic lights, elevators, air-conditioning systems, lighting systems, surveillance systems. All of these systems depend on electrical energy. In a smart grid system based on diffused sensors such as the IoT, these systems will be connected to the web and rely on it. For electrical energy, for connection, and their management.

The Internet of Things' system will develop exponentially, and the problem of security and users' privacy will become impeding. Though, if we give the problem the proper attention, IoT will become a crucial enabler

for developing a new paradigm for all the necessary services of a smart city.
Goal 7, as we said, can be faced thanks to the smart grid systems, and **Goal 6:** *Ensure availability and sustainable management of water and sanitation for all* can be achieved using IoT sensors to create smart waterworks in towns. Optimizing our resources, avoiding water waste, and monitoring water health. For example, this is happening in Stockholm, where Ericsson, from 2017, started a project for the development of a monitoring system on the city water network. The system analyses water purity and allows checks and real-time interventions on targeted areas of the water network if any contamination should be found[204].

Moving towards **Goal 12:** *Ensure sustainable consumption and production patterns*, the Internet of Things becomes vital for fulfilling some of the targets, such as eco-friendly waste management.[205] The small prices of the sensors, together with the new generation communication network (think about the 5G), allow managing the waste life cycle in its full length. IoT-equipped dustbins are taking hold in many towns. They possess centralized waste management systems to enhance especially their recycling efficiency. When the bin is full, the sensors will communicate on the Net the necessity of collection. TIM, for example, inside the project Replicate, implemented IoT sensors to monitor the dustbins' filling and optimize the waste collection in Florence. The smart bin knows when it is full and books a collection so that the truck can optimize its route. The Japanese enterprise Fujitsu, using the same logic, developed a smart bin to manage the recycling of electronic waste: on average, each collection bin avoids the release of one ton of waste per year in dumps.

---

[204] The project is part of the Digital Demo Stockholm Initiative, aiming at making Stockholm the smartest town in the world by 2040.
[205] In particular:

- **Target 12.4**: By 2020, achieve the environmentally sound management of chemicals and all wastes throughout their life cycle, in accordance with agreed international frameworks, and significantly reduce their release to air, water and soil in order to minimize their adverse impacts on human health and the environment
- **Target 12.5**: By 2030, substantially reduce waste generation through prevention, reduction, recycling and reuse.

Again: thanks to the Internet of Things, we could develop constant monitoring systems for the natural areas, preventing catastrophic climate events and pre-alerting local authorities and population. Memory goes back to 2004 when 230.000 people died, and half a million were dispersed because of the terrible tsunami that hit 14 countries of the Pacific Ocean. Every year thousands of people die because of these catastrophes. The achievement of **Goal 13:** *Take urgent action to combat climate change and its impacts* needs the implementation of IoT systems. In Colombia, for example, a network of solar energy powered sensors was installed next to the river Liboriana. The sensors should help reduce the risk of floods and overflowing. The sensors monitor the situation continuously, and they send a series of warnings automatically. If a threat is detected, sirens are activated, local and municipal authorities are alerted, and text messages are sent (through instant messaging systems like WhatsApp, as well) automatically. The data are stored in the cloud to allow the research centers and authorities full access to conduct studies, researches, and previsions.

The list could be endless, mentioning applications for forest management, fish shipment, and the security and monitoring of the food industries. In conclusion: the Internet of Things tore down the wall between the analogic and the digital and created a universe in which these two worlds, separated at first, now merge, redefining economic models, social paradigms, behavioral patterns.

Intersections

The demolition of the wall between real and virtual saw, with social network sites' birth, the beginning of a merging path of the physical and digital universes. The Internet of Things finds its place, finally closing the circle. It is more and more difficult to imagine these two worlds as separate. In our reality today, the physical and digital worlds are interpenetrated so profoundly that it is useless and impossible to divide them.

This is a real Möbius[206] loop, in which the two sides, analogic and digital, define a single surface, represented by reality, our life.

It is not a coincidence that the technologies developing faster encompass both sides of the loop in a time of such agitated changes, contributing to demolishing the last delicate walls. They will create a model for the future in which it will be impossible (and useless) to make distinctions.

We still need to take into serious consideration the social and economic changes (and also changes regarding the private sphere from a cognitive, psychological, and anthropological point of view), but we need to set coherent questions, to take the right direction and not hit the concrete and high wall of reality. Depicting the web as a hikikomori[207] maker will only make it like that. Auto-isolated people are an extreme example, and they need treatment like any other pathology. We do not have to demonize this device that already changed our existence; instead, we need to think carefully about the balancing process between the positive and negative aspects to make the firsts prevail over the seconds.

In our hyperconnected world, the so-called intersection technologies between digital and analogic are growing. We are talking about all those technologies that facilitate and smooth the shift between the two contexts.

We are in the robotics age, trying to give arms and legs (or better, wheels, sensors, and servomotors) to the artificial intelligence systems, enabling them to go beyond the limit of the digital and interact with the objects of the world of the atoms. It makes no sense to consider them as two opposite universes. These universes were often created by the fantasy of sci-fi writers, the same that created the bad robot, ready to take men's place and rule over them. An unlikely scenario, at least during our existence

---

[206] The Mobius's loop or string is a surface with two sides and one surface that inspired the Dutch lithographer and engraver Maurits Cornelis Escher's art. It is used many times in his works.

[207] The Japanese term describes the auto-isolated (from hiku "throw" and komoru "retreat"): these people never leave their home to handle every relations through the web.

and our children's, and their children's, but it depicts too well the difficulty of humankind to relate with machines.

These machines can be used, from this very moment, to produce well-being. At the dawning of the robotization age, we need to set precise rules that will be the outcome of a serious and shared reflection outlining roles, goals, ties, opportunities, and threats. In this age, we need to keep in our minds, more than ever, that the difference between Taylorism and Fordism is not about technologies, identical for both models, but about the way they are employed.

Today, we have machines that engineer other machines; that is why we need to fix the designing criteria. In light of a sustainable world, these criteria need to follow the scheme of Agenda 2030.

We already have many examples of possible applications. Think about **Goal 2**: *End hunger, achieve food security, and improved nutrition and promote sustainable agriculture.* Robotics, together with IoT and artificial intelligence, is already revolutionizing agriculture. Smart farming allows the management of vast areas with low costs, allowing the development of agriculture in places where otherwise it would not have been economically sustainable.[208] It also decreased the use of pesticides and fertilizers, supporting the fulfillment of **Goal 3**: *Ensure healthy lives and promote well-being for all at all ages*[209]. Physics, information science, and electronics are formidable allies to decrease the use of chemicals in the fields. In farming and many other sectors such as industry, Robotics is not the cause for job contraction. The economic models based on the exploitation of labor are the real cause. That is why we need to foster new models based on the cooperation of men and machines, according to **Goal 8:** *Promote sustained, inclusive and sustainable economic growth, full and productive employment and decent work for all.* Thinking that robots and artificial intelligence will destroy jobs is like thinking that Ned Ludd's loom was an ominous invention. If we ask a workman his opinion about the robots exoskeletons used in storehouses to decrease the muscular

---

[208] AA. VV. The future of food and agriculture, trends and challenges, FAO, 2017

[209] In particual **Target 3.9**: *By 2030, substantially reduce the number of deaths and illnesses from hazardous chemicals and air, water and soil pollution and contamination*

strain, we realize it is not true that technology brings poverty, excluding people from their jobs. Technology changes work. That is true. The apocalyptic side blames it for killing work. Data contradicts this belief, showing that technology – at the most – can be the enabling instrument of economic and social models that can increase unemployment in the name of profit. That is why economic development, and consequently, technological development, need to inspire themselves to society models based on sustainability.

According to their business model, our nurseryman Domenico or our cheese-businesswoman Anna cannot hire a high number of people anyway. Robotics does not cause their employees to be fired; on the other hand, it eases their daily fatigue allowing them to manage their activities sustainably.

We realize that robotics is not something created to exclude people from the labor world; on the contrary, it is an instrument that eases the strain.

It helps people in the management of extreme situations. Thanks to smart, intelligent, and independent drones, it allows us to carry out all those jobs too dangerous for men. And also give men the arms to reach what they can not—for example, the many applications in the health care sector. Sometimes surgery requires such precision that the help of a robotic system is needed. Thanks to robotics, and the high-speed Net, the same surgeon can also operate thousands of miles away from his patient. (from a different perspective, this helps the development of **Goal 3**: *Ensure healthy lives and promote well-being for all at all ages.)*

Every sector is reached by robotics, but what happens when we need to put into action something that was created in a digital context? Literally, if we mean a physical form dealing with the intersections between digital and analogic, then it becomes essential to resort to additive manufacturing, commonly known as 3D printing.
Additive manufacturing has the same impacts on the production processes as Gutemberg's inventions had on the printing processes.

With the expression additive manufacturing, we refer to how an object is printed by a device: the 3D printer. It overlaps thin layers of material, welding and blending them, producing all sorts of complex shapes. Several materials can be used: from polymers (plastic, artificial resin, biopolymers) to metals: (steel, titanium, bronze, noble metals), allowing various applications. 3D printing can simplify the 'prototypization' and support the production of small series of objects or single objects. In conclusion, any conceivable and drawable geometry, structurally achievable with solid modeling software, can be printed (with all due respect to Escher). The application fields are varied: from craftsmanship to biomedicine, from gold working to gastronomy, from architecture to the construction industry. Some 3D printers work at molecular levels, and others are so big to print – literally – entire houses.

The 3D printing engenders significant economic impacts, representing, for the production processes, what the cloud represented for services. It enabled the small-sized industries to develop new activities, not achievable before because they would have meant bigger industrial facilities. It opened new worlds.

Some 3D printers are used to print 3D printers, recursively, starting from a single printer to almost any possible material object.

Referring to **Goal 3**: *Ensure healthy lives and promote well-being for all at all ages,* we are now experimenting with biological 3D printers. They could be used to print entire body organs, built on the base of the patient's DNA, and thus removing all the possible risks of rejection. Today, many doctors like Carla can use printers to produce artificial limbs, the replacement of bones explicitly designed on each patient's morphology, characteristics, and dimensions. These prosthetics can be printed in every part of the world; it was not even conceivable to craft customized implants in those areas before. Not to mention the achievable results by combining 3D printing, robotics, and artificial intelligence. For example, the Sant'Anna Institution in Pisa, through the *spinoff* Prensilia, produced Mia, a robotic hand and arm prosthetic, permanently implanted on a human being thanks to osseointegration.

The human being started from the first computer programs through which he arrives at physical objects' production. Soon, we arrive at the successors of those programs: complex systems of artificial intelligence algorithms that produce not only items but also biological tissues. There would be much more to be imagined if we were sci-fi novelists, but what we can do with present technologies is already noteworthy.

In Amsterdam, for example, every citizen has been evaluated to produce, on average, 23 kilos of plastics, so they decided to start the project Print your City. This project, resorting to the big 3D printers, produces urban décor objects using the plastics delivered by the citizens. The plastics produced by two citizens is enough to make the polymeric fiber to print a bench. Print your City is a project wholly inspired by environmental sustainability and the principles of the circular economy. It also aims to involve the community and the factories, encourage the purchase of these benches, and the application of the industry's logo on them, activating participation chain, applying on the objects the names of the people who contributed to making the object. And last but not least, the project shows how plastic can be something more than an ecologic monster if used with responsibility and managed through all its life cycle. It is indeed an intelligent way to deal with several of the goals described by Agenda 2030, all at once. From the battle for the health of **Goal 3**: *Ensure healthy lives and promote well-being for all at all ages*[210] to the development of sustainable human settlements described by **Goal 11:** *Make cities and human settlements inclusive, safe, resilient and sustainable,*[211] from the fight against pollution of **Goal** ***12:*** *Ensure sustainable consumption and production patterns*[212] to oceans safeguard of ***Goal 14:*** *Conserve and*

---

[210] In particular **Target 3.9**: *By 2030, substantially reduce the number of deaths and illnesses from hazardous chemicals and air, water and soil pollution and contamination*

[211] In particular:

- **Target 11.3**: *By 2030, enhance inclusive and sustainable urbanization and capacity for participatory, integrated and sustainable human settlement planning and management in all countries*
- **Target 11.6**: *By 2030, reduce the adverse per capita environmental impact of cities, including by paying special attention to air quality and municipal and other waste management*

[212] In particular **Target 12.5**: *By 2030, substantially reduce waste generation through prevention, reduction, recycling and reuse*

sustainably use the oceans, seas and marine resources for sustainable development.[213]
It is clear – out of any doubt – that sustainability connects all the different complex systems of our reality. Every socially sustainable behavior engenders an economically favorable reaction, and it has a positive impact on the environment.

Artificial intelligence allows the programs to learn; robotics allows the programs to go beyond their digital limit and reach the material world. The Internet of Things allows every object to become a smart object, and – to close the circle –3D printing allows printing anything a software can represent. From this perspective, it is clear that looking at the digital as something different from reality, something to be locked up in a computer is entirely out of line and out of time.

And if it is not enough, even the interaction patterns developed between the human being and the *devices* around him show how we are all going towards a direction of integration between physical and immaterial, in a real analogic reality "augmented" by the digital.

In the beginning, before the fourth industrial revolution had started, the attention was focused on the possible reproduction in a digital context of all the spaces, settings, and relations typical of the analogic world. It was the age of that virtual reality described in films such as Tron[214]or The Lawnmower Man,[215]and later, platforms such as Second Life in which the user could plunge into a second virtual life.

Virtual reality is then the digital reproduction of a material universe. The user is completely "absorbed," sometimes using instruments such as 3D glasses, allowing him to live realistic situations. Apart from recreational

---

[213] In particular: **target 14.1:** *By 2025, prevent and significantly reduce marine pollution of all kinds, in particular from land-based activities, including marine debris and nutrient pollution*

[214] Tron is a movie produced in 1982 and directed by Steven Lisberger. It was produced by Walt Disney and it is the first film to focus on virtual reality. It is also the first film to use computer graphics.

[215] The Lawnmower man is a film produced in 1992 directed by Brett Leonard and deals with virtual reality.

applications, virtual reality can be used in most various fields. In designing and architecture, it is possible to move in tridimensional settings before their creation to understand their efficiency better; in tourism, one can visit a place without leaving their home; in medical education, a doctor like Carla can train for surgery using perfectly 3D reproduced organs; and taxi drivers like Alfio can improve their driving performances through safe drive courses with no actual risk. The list could be even longer, and many of the applications have possible feasibility in the light of Agenda 2030's goals.
The Virtual Human Interaction Lab of Standford University, for example, has been working since 2017 on a series of projects focused on people's sensibilization about environmental pollution. The project plans to build immersive experiences in which the participants are involved in situations depicting the effects of pollution. To explain the impact of oceans' acidification, they used the coral bay of Ischia Isle. For the same purposes, the NGO AnimalEquaity produced a series of immersive videos in which the user experiences intensive animal farming from the victims' point of view: the animals. These examples show how virtual reality can be used – crossing the goals of Agenda 2030 – to support a sensibilization process on its goals.

Concretely, virtual reality is used for education in all the critical contexts where people need to act in an emergency or potential threat situations. For example, doctors like Carla or technicians acting on complex and delicate systems (power or water plants, engines, etc.). In this sense, the contribution for the fulfillment o
Virtual reality can be a strong ally in the fight against discrimination. Referred to **Goal 5:** *Achieve gender equality and empower all women and girls*. The solutions offered by BeAnotherLab are particularly interesting. Neuroscience researchers underlined how it is possible to create cognitive illusions that will give the impression of feeling other people's emotions. This condition is called *full body ownership illusion*. The psychological and physiological responses suggest how people would feel in a different body. Using virtual reality techniques, the users are directly involved in other people's lives and stories, experiencing racism or gender inequalities. Another startup, the Rendever in Boston, used the same approach to work in senior centers and created positive shared experiences

thanks to virtual reality. The group sessions allow the elderly, particularly the ill that cannot leave their rooms, to experience fun, movement, and wonder, only wearing a viewer. The same goes for another startup, the NomadVR in Sidney, offering assistance to elderly and disabled people, making day trips based on virtual reality. This system allows the elderly and the people living with them to continue exploring the world and visiting new places and relatives otherwise impossible to reach. Far from being a virtual contribution, it helps develop **Goal 3**: *Ensure healthy lives and promote well-being for all at all ages.*

Goal 16: *Promote peaceful and inclusive societies for sustainable development, provide access to justice for all and build effective, accountable and inclusive institutions at all levels.* Shared Studios is inspired by goal 16 and uses the same overmentioned models. The Brooklyn factory is the major in producing immersive environments and uses its expertise to develop virtual reality spaces in which the users are plunged into Afghanistan, Iraq, or Mexico and interact with the locals in a realistic context. The purpose is to connect different people from different worlds, to get to know each other, and start a pacific dialog.

If virtual reality is an attempt to rebuild the material world in an immaterial dimension, then the solutions based on the augmented reality are of particular interest, according to the intersections between the first and the second.

With the expression augmented reality, we refer to the possibility to enrich the experiences in physical contexts with digital information. Resorting to the most popular devices in our daily life – from the omnipresent smartphones to the smartwatches and the smartglasses[216] - the augmented reality is a technique that allows overlapping real-time digital information on images of the real world. With augmented reality, one can look at a monument, know its name, and have further information with the interactive device. The same goes for route maps, the brands of objects, or their functioning. Even people's names. This particular point

[216] Smartglasses are glasses that allow to overlap data and information on the owner's visual field thanks to interactive lenses.

raised some perplexities, culminating in a real social denial for the items (like the smart glasses) that allowed such a deep and violent intrusion of the digital in real life. One thing is looking at an object through a smartphone's camera; another is to look at a person with your glasses and acquire information on their name directly on the lenses. To safeguard what's left of our privacy, they decided not to develop applications for facial identification. The intrusiveness of augmented reality in the over-mentioned contexts is, of course, a limit and an issue to take into account, but it is undeniable that it offers excellent advantages in different fields, from marketing to logistics, from education to security.

Referring to Agenda 2030, it is immediate to think about emergency interventions in highly dangerous contexts. Thanks to augmented reality, the operators can have real-time support from remote experts or information on what they are facing before dealing with it. For example, General Electrics is employing augmented reality for its activities to give its workers information in the right moment, in the most suitable format, directly in their visual field, and with bare hands. This optimizes labor time, reduces the risks for workers, and contributes to creating sustainable work dynamics. Lockheed Martin adopted the AR Hololens released by Microsoft for the production of space shuttles. The Lockheed technicians can use the images cast on the lenses to identify and label the positions of the hundreds of elements they deal with, decreasing the intervention times by one order of magnitude. Both cases are concrete contributions for achieving **Goal 8**: *Promote sustained, inclusive and sustainable economic growth, full and productive employment, and decent work for all.*

Augmented reality towards **Goal 3**: *Ensure healthy lives and promote well-being for all at all ages* can be an essential support in the treatment of specific pathologies. The researchers of Keck School of Medicine of the University of California[217], for example, verified that in cases of retinitis pigmentosa, a genetic disorder of the eyes that causes loss of vision, the augmented reality systems can effectively improve the patients' mobility and their performances, and of course their life. The system developed

[217] A. N. Angelopoulos, H. Ameri, D. Mitra, M. Humayun. Enhanced Depth Navigation Through Augmented Reality Depth Mapping in Patients with Low Vision, Nature, 2019.

by The University of California overlaps objects inside a wireframe with four bright and different colors. In this way, the glasses supply chromatic visual inputs that help people with tunnel vision understand complex environments or avoid obstacles in scarcely lit places.

The future in our choices

Defining what is what and what society will be is not up to technologies, but it will rest on humankind and how it will decide to implement them. This is digital sustainability, in essence. We are facing today a responsibility that encompasses institutions as well as individuals: to make choices that will change the future of the world. These choices are not only a governments' matter because the building of a sustainable future starts from an individual sensibilization as well as a collective dimension. Not only to answer the need for awareness but also to face the concrete impacts that sustainable development – or its absence – generates in everyone.

This book started with Valerio's voice, a young journalist that back in the '80s was undertaking his career – and his life – with enthusiasm and passion. Then his life turned into a (hopefully) dystopic future, in which his profession was subdued to a creepy artificial intelligence that – to explode the myth that artificial intelligence is a threat to repetitive jobs only – completely replaced journalists. Moreover, Valerio thinks, staring at a silent sea because devoid of any life. In Valerio's world and life, everything went wrong. That is because we could not understand what technologies promised to do and see the threats to minimize them to highlight the opportunities. Valerio's story is a story of big choices concerning themes as artificial intelligence and the environment's future. There are other stories of those who face the future with optimism and a bit of ignorance. That is Alfio's story. The taxi driver, regardless of his difficult life, is convinced that the future always has an opportunity in store. That is why he decides to take a taxi license in the worst moment ever: his job si endangered by the development of economic systems that, thanks to technologies, will change the value chain in his sector. The individual dimension overlaps the social one: how do we act to empower technological development and make it an economic and social driver? How do we act not to hinder technology in favor of those who would be damaged by its development?. The Red Flag Act's story – the laws that imposed to have a warner announcing the arrival of a car when traveling to London – is significant. We need to ask ourselves how many Red Flag Acts we have in our law in our behaviors in our business strategies. The role of institutions is to foster social development, but sustainable development means safeguarding all those endangered by it. Supporting the development and also who bears the brunt of it. We know it is a failure, though, to unite the two phases and start facing the second one.

On the other hand, riding the wave of progress and adjusting to the change is not easy. Carla is our example. She is a skillful doctor, but she cannot stand the idea that a computer system could enhance her performance. Living the relationship between humans and artificial intelligence in a contrast dimension is comprehensible, but it is a mistake our society cannot afford. The reality is so complex, and its complexity is growing by the day that technology's support is fundamental. Refusing technology would mean making us inappropriate to face this world, becoming the victims, paradoxically. Including technology in our behaviors, in our routines, in our activities means to understand it, redefine it, take advantage of it to produce positive outcomes. The future is not people versus machines; it is people using machines to improve their lives.

Like Anna and Domenico, the cheesemaker and the nurseryman. Two figures able to intercept the direction of change, understand its potential advantages, and pick the opportunities in their work. Anna and Domenico embody what we should be and what society could become if we understand the importance of sustainable development promoted by the United Nations through Agenda 2030. In Anna and Domenico's stories, there are two main obstacles that the innovators need to face: with Anna, we face the resistance to change. Her choices are opposed by her family, the founders of the factory, even the employees. Tradition is just a trench against the new and a shield to hide the fear. These factors have a devastating impact on society because they reinforce the individual and collective comfort zones. They run the risk to take into consideration only the negative aspects of technological development, which, however, is inevitable. With Domenico, we witness the so-called innovator's solitude.

His reflections hit him while he is wandering, lonely, through his greenhouses. Innovation is the result of a collective process, but the innovator is often alone in this collective process. It is in its nature that the starting point is to be faced with loneliness. Often, like in Anna's case, we are alone against those who do not understand innovation or do not want to. However, Anna and Domenico are living proof that the road to innovation is not only possible but also the only option.

04.

The choices for digital sustainability

Choosing digital sustainability

Environment, society, economy, no matter where we start, these elements are deeply linked, interconnected, and interdependent. The building of a sustainable future, avoiding any one-sided fundamentalism, depends on balancing the resources (economic, environmental, social) to build a development model focusing on the human being in full respect for himself and the environment, which will be his legacy for future generations.
In this context, complex but not complicated, technology – digital technology in particular – takes on a fundamental role. In the development process of which we are protagonists, technology embodies both the object and the subject of the ongoing development path; that is why its role is even more delicate.
Technology – as an object – is the instrument of change: through technology, we determine the economic, social, and environmental change patterns, in an articulate system of dependencies between technology itself and the phenomena engendered by it and that, in their turn, engender it.
Digital technology is an instrument of change with so crucial a role to contribute to the definition of the developments, but it is also the subject because the choices we make fall on it, defining the substance of the overmentioned developments and even its nature and its structure.

In both cases, the concept of choice is vital.

On the one hand, being the object, the choices about it will define its function for social, economic, and environmental sustainability. On the other hand, being the subject, its nature will be profoundly influenced by our choices, which will redefine its sense and perspective and reshape the concepts of sustainability concerning it.

Choosing digital technology's role will be functional to make it an instrument of sustainability and give it a sustainable dimension. In other words, in the years to come, we will make choices regarding technology. These choices will determine how it will be useful for sustainable development and the fact that it will be sustainable itself.

Digital sustainability, in this sense, behaves like the other social, economic, and environmental elements. They are characterized by a self-functional dimension and by a dimension functional to the other elements to which they are related.

Digital sustainability, as well, behaves like a sub-system of a more complex system. But, more than the others – because of its transversal element – it is functional to the development of the social, environmental, and economic systems. It is clear that when we talk about environmental, social, and economic sustainability, we also need to take into consideration digital sustainability. Including in the expression everything regarding the digital system's choices, the impacts on its development model, and the other systems'.

Digital sustainability is the one defining the development patterns of digital technology to create a better world, according to its nature and its instrumental role in society, economy, and environment.

It will be fundamental to answer a series of questions that will substantiate the role of digital from a sustainability point of view in both dimensions. We need to keep in mind that the answers are not already prepared, and the choices will implicate – to balance risks and opportunities – sacrifices. The choices often will come from a polarized dimension, but they will find the ideal dimension in the balance between the two.

What will be the big choices that technology dictates for the building of a sustainable world? In other words, what are (some of) the choices that will define our future?

Real or virtual?

It may seem the mother of all choices about the relation of human beings and digital technology. Actually, it is the first on our list not because it is the most important, but because it is the first to overcome.

All the distinctions between the two dimensions of reality are born from the dichotomy of real and virtual: analogic and digital, material and immaterial, online and offline. Each difference, from a particular perspective, aims at describing juxtaposed universes and gives them value. Juxtaposition inevitably arises both negative and positive values. It is like a team game, in which the supporters try to defend their own team, more than trying to understand the evolution of a phenomenon. It has been decades, but we still have not come to terms with the distinction between apocalyptics and integrated, not realizing that the opposite word for real is unreal, not virtual. This substitution only urges the belief that virtual means, simply, unreal.

The choice between real and virtual, despite the strains of the apocalyptic and the resistance of the integrated, has no sense, especially in a context where they will be more and more permeated. In the actual world, where information science went beyond the limit of a computer to enter the objects, and people can – and will more and more – move inside unlimited virtual spaces, with wider juxtaposition margins between the two contexts, it makes no sense to ask what is real and what is virtual.

Today, the reality is already both analogic and digital, and any dichotomy strains to keep alive. Think about the purchase process: when do we decide what to buy? When someone talks about a product at the bar or when a friend of ours writes a review on the social network? When we see it in a shop or when we watch a video online? When we talk to a shop assistant or when we discuss it in a forum? And the same goes for opinions about people, our holiday choice, and our vote for the elections. We lost the ability to distinguish the origin of the elicitations that influence our choices. We did so because this ability – for the user – is entirely useless. For better or for worse, digital devices are profoundly redefining the sense of many concepts. The result will be a variation of sense, sprung in a world where the difference between real and virtual – especially for young generations – will be more and more blurred.

In this dimension, the next big step of information science is remarkably coherent. It will witness, thanks to quantum computing, the passing of the dichotomy limits of the digital.
There will be a moment in which digital information science will not express strict alternatives based on zero and one anymore. It will be the expression of concurrent contemporaneity with quantum information science, and maybe the distinction between real and virtual will be automatically overcome.

Until then, society needs to rearrange the meaning of the concepts of real and virtual. Giving the real a new sense: the place in which physical and immaterial contexts redefine our model of interactions with other people, with information, with the world around us. And looking at the shared root of the two words virtual and virtue, we need to remember that the digital can make the world better, more sustainable, nurture progress that allows real improvement of individual living conditions and growth in society's awareness.

The dichotomy between real and virtual brings us to reflect on defensive models instead of integration schemes. Only if we try to go beyond this dichotomy will society be ready to orient towards the real dichotomy it will have to face.

Security or freedom?

If the distinction between real and virtual is destined to disappear, the one between security and freedom is another story. In the name of this choice, related to the role of technology in society and the ways it would and could develop, we will make the decisions that will have the greatest impacts on people and populations.

The balancing is far from simple. It needs to be interpreted in the double dimension of object and subject, in which the aspects are strictly related: on one side, the free Web, on the other, the Web as an instrument of freedom. The same, in juxtaposition, the safe Web and the Web as an instrument of security.

In each of its interpretations, freedom has been one of the most powerful driving force for the development of the Web. From its origin, the internet was considered an instrument of freedom. It is undeniable it contributed to the development of a more open society. Open to confront with diversity, to knowing new things, to access everything out of the self. The internet is an instrument of knowledge and openness; it is the place for confrontation and growth. It granted access to information and consequently to knowledge and awareness. From awareness springs the ability to understand one's own rights and fight for them. It is no coincidence that the United Nations defined the Web as an inalienable right. Not based on its recreational and entertainment dimensions, or because it can be used to enjoy services, but because it is an instrument of knowledge and a means to exert one's rights.

In this sense, the two interpretations of the concept of freedom – the internet as a free Web and the internet as an instrument of freedom – tend to coincide: there are no elements in contrast. Or, at least, those who witnessed the birth of the internet want to read it like this and will continue to read it like this, thinking about the Web of the future.

In essence, the free and open dimension of the internet, which must not be mistaken with an anarchic dimension (even in its structure, the Web is based on strict rules and protocols, guaranteeing its efficiency), also allows it to be an instrument of freedom.

However, its characteristics also allow the development of a Web made of underground connections, eluding the research engines and also the authorities, potentially transforming the Web into an instrument to break the law.

It is the realm of the *deep Web* and the *dark Web*[218].

And so the distinction between the Web as a context (whose freedom must be granted) and the Web as an instrument (of freedom) starts to be relevant.

Let us start from the first point: how can we act to guarantee that the Net – being free – is also safe for those who surf it? Freedom and security are two domains naturally opposing each other. The more a system is free and open – a technological, economic, or social system – the less it is safe. The more a system is closed and regulated, the better it can be made safe. Here the first part of the problem comes into play. It is one of the main topics discussed by the Internet Governance Forum since 2006. This multilateral forum fostered by the Secretary-General of the United Nations aims to create informal open groups for the elaboration of recommendations.

---

[218] With the expression deep web, we mean that part of the internet contents which is not trackable through the browsers. The reason is the technological difficulty of the operation, performed by the software so-called "crawlers" on Google's behalf. They continuously scan the new web contents to index them. Not to be confused with the dark web, that is a part of the deep web made of those who deliberately decide to "hide" their contents from the web for illegal purposes, mainly.

The problem is not (only) about the law. If it is true that we are living in a world where the difference between virtual and real is going to fade, then it is also true that a "Web law" has no sense. What we need with urgency is a law that takes into consideration the impacts of the Web on society, people, and the economy. It is crucial to the role of supranational organisms because it has no sense to think about national law projects in a context that is, by definition, devoid of any barrier.

To have a safe web, it is necessary, as a first thing, to act on the cultural dimension, and only then to define rules and schemes in a supranational context. To guarantee security, how much will these schemes undermine the internet's freedom? Even more important: how much is the freedom of the Web functional for a better and more sustainable future? To find the right balance, it is unavoidable to look at freedom and security issues from a sustainable point of view, referring to the Goals of Agenda 2030, the beacon for decision-making.

The question is still open, and the answer is bloody complex. Because the countries' tendency, especially when they see the internet as a potential threat, is to limit freedom in favor of security. It is important to keep in mind that every step behind, in favor of security over freedom, needs great effort to be traveled through again. Moreover, one never understands the value of that bit of freedom until it is lost. And it will cost great efforts to get it back.

This process is clear if we think about concrete problems. Think about the spread of hate speech[219]. This phenomenon finds a breeding ground in the perception of impunity of those hiding behind a monitor. This phenomenon is similar to what happens when we are driving our car, and someone overtakes us: the violence with which we address the unaware driver is different from the reaction we would have if we were outside the shelter of our cabin.

---

[219] With this expression we mean all those hostile content and communication activities against individuals or communities. The Encyclopedia Britannica explains: speech or expression that denigrates a person or persons on the basis of (alleged) membership in a social group identified by attributes such as race, ethnicity, gender, sexual orientation, religion, age, physical or mental disability, and others.

Hate speech is born as a result of scarce knowledge of the instrument and its characteristics. Often it is a symptom of ignorance (about the instrument and not only). It is clear that this phenomenon needs to be stopped. The solution, which is not easy, is to act on the cultural lever. Giving users the right cultural and cognitive instruments, we hope they will be responsible and conscious.
One of the suggested solutions – rapid and useless – is the users' filing. In other words, the user is being asked to register using their ID and submitting their data to the owner of the service's control. This solution is technically faulty, but also, even if it were possible, it would mean that every user, to be online, had to give personal data to a commerce operator, entrusting it with the dangerous responsibility (out of its competence) of managing personal information.

It would be the end of the "pseudo-anonymity" on the Web. The prefix 'pseudo' refers to the fact that when a user connects to the internet, he leaves many traces. Such as the numbers of the telephone and the device he is using to connect. It means that the authorities – with the operators' cooperation – can track the author. In this context, without the cooperation between operators and authorities by means of the D.A., no one can reach the user. The separation of the role is not secondary nor banal because it protects the users, even if they are trackable, should they commit a crime.

Losing the right to anonymity is not a solution, and mass filing would be like imposing every user to wear a public label displaying his data whenever he goes walking on the streets. Would this action make cities safer? It is unlikely. But surely it would make citizens less free, shifting the security management issue from the Government to the citizen. In this framework, we need to take into account the risks to surrender the citizens' data. Generic risks, if connected to commercial management, but very concrete if connected to a specific situation. For example, if there were a data leak – as it has already happened – by the hand of hackers, or only for malfunctioning: what would happen to the victims of stalking, reachable by their stalkers? What would happen to those people that, for any personal and justified reasons, do not want to disclose information on their life, their living place, their contacts?

It is not by chance that all those working on human rights be horrified by the idea of a bill concerning the filing of social media users. The bill would demand – in the name of security – the users to surrender their freedom. The freedom to give personal documents to an operator that could lose them, give them to third parties, or misuse them. Not to mention what would happen in repressive or authoritarian Governments.

This point underlines the importance of the second part of the problem: using the internet as an instrument of freedom or security. Renouncing freedom over security threatens to make the Web a great repressive instrument instead of a freedom instrument.

It is the case in China, where there is a system called *social scoring*. Every user has a personal score, and he will gain or lose points according to his online and offline behaviors, monitoring every daily activity. Is he fined for speeding? He loses points, but it is not a problem. Does he speak ill of the governments? He loses points. And this can also cause some issues.

It is for lack of true anonymity that we need to defend the Web's freedom because the internet must not become a repressive instrument in the name of security. To avoid any surveillance dictatorship, we need to fight any attempt to reduce freedom.

In the next future, society will have to decide how much freedom and how much security to be granted on the Web and when protecting over the other. The choice, however, will not be presented in these terms.

We will have to face, step by step, specific matters, superficially limited and secondary, in which the apparent increase of security will be compensated by what will be felt like a small and insignificant decrease in freedom.

That is why we need a great spread consciousness, to be sure that every player perceives the game's dimension at stake.

Privacy or control?

If the balance between freedom and security is a matter between a State and its citizens, there is another element of choice that will have a great impact on our lives: the concepts of privacy and control. This relation does not (only) concern the relationship between a country and the citizen but also (and above all) between users and services providers.

To fully understand the complexity of this relationship, it is necessary to analyze the evolution of the concept of privacy. It is also important to refer to the tangible impact of what has been called by the economist Shoshana Zuboff – with an apocalyptic but particularly appropriate metaphor – surveillance capitalism[220].
The problem, in the end, is focused on a straightforward question. We live in the Internet of Things and artificial intelligence age. We live in the confluence of big data and social networks, with billions of connected objects speaking to each other and us, managed by a small number of actors: the platforms. With a business plan, the platform is based on the accurate knowledge of users' characteristics, tastes, and choices. What will the impacts of this ecosystem on our privacy be and, consequently, the quality of our lives? And again, what will the right balance between the possibility for the user to keep his privacy and the possibility for the operators to use the information produced by the users whenever they access a free service (only apparently free, actually he is paying with the value of his data) be? In building an economic and social model based on sustainability principles, what will the limit between privacy protection and access to a service ecosystem connected to daily routine management?

---

[220]S. Zuboff, The Age of surveillance capitalism. The fight for a human future at the new frontier of power, profile Books Ltd, 2019

In this scenario, apocalyptic visions mingle with integrated visions. On one side, the "cyber optimistic," such as Clay Shirky,[221] essayist, and professor at New York University, praising a connected world. On the other, the Belarussian specialist Evgenij Morozov, sounding the alarm against those defined as the owners of the Net: social network sites, search engines, new intermediaries and in general the multinational companies basing their business model on the users' data, and gaining more and more economical and social power.

The situation is complicated, but it gets even more complicated because if we want to understand its dynamics, we need to frame the characteristics of the concept of privacy. This concept has changed over the years, and the moment we try to define it, it keeps changing exponentially. The risk is that while we analyze the concept, it has already changed, and we are reflecting on something outdated. The risk is even greater, considering that we tend to observe some social phenomena forgetting that the perspective – Heisenberg teaches – influences inexorably what we look at and also who is watching.

In this case, a picture of society in its relationship with privacy, taken from one and only perspective (our perspective), is not enough. We need a film tracing the evolution of the concept over time. Only by watching this film, we realize how deeply the concept of privacy has changed. One of the most fascinating and famous definitions of Warren and Brandeis's American jurists is "the right to be alone." It was 1890, and that right was born from the need to be protected from the daily press, which was developing fast. It is not a coincidence that the attention on the matter of privacy increases exponentially whenever a phenomenon – the press then, the social media and the Internet of Things now – risks to undermine what should be an individual right. Actually, it varies profoundly from age to age in the perception of its importance.

---

[221]C. Shirky, Here Comes Everybody, the power of organizing without organization, Penguin Press, 2008

What are the dimensions of this change? Suffice to think about the architecture to understand. We need to wait until the second half of the Eighteenth Century for the corridors to be introduced in our houses. Before then, it was quite normal for people to cross every single room to move from one side of the house to another. In each room, the residents were carrying out their daily activities: eating, sleeping, washing. This architectural style evened out peasants' houses and lords' houses. The historians tell that Madame de Maintenon slept in the same room used by Louis XIV to meet his ministers: "while the king is debating, the chambermaids undress her and help her going to bed." It was nothing strange if we think that the Sun King was used to receive his guests seated on a commode (which was not precisely a chair).

Are Social media and the Internet of Things taking us back to Bourbon, France? Maybe the setting is a bit different, but we are again in a big house with no corridors where anyone – potentially – can make their room public with a click. The born-digital is used to it: more than a third of their accounts on social network sites are public: they are devoid of any protection from indiscreet gazes. The real problem is to understand if that is the result of a conscious choice or only the result of a matter of fact arising from unawareness of what is at stake. The stake is directly proportional to the data's value and grows exponentially with its availability on the Web.

We need to pay attention: the lower perception of a right's importance does not decrease its practical value. On the contrary: the more we lose awareness, the better it needs to be safeguarded. It is certain that during the Sun King's age, it was possible, if needed, to be left alone. Can we say the same today? The risk of living in a house without corridors is real: that is why we need to be able to close the doors.

The platforms have all the interests in owning the keys of these doors.

That is why we are talking about "surveillance capitalism": the platforms' profit is strictly dependent on their ability to continuously watch over their users and extract value from this surveillance. This value springs from the control over the users who generated it. From this value derives

the profit of those who offer the services. These services, far from being free, are paid with the value of their data.
If it is true that, how Henry David Thoreau used to say: "The price of anything is the amount of life you exchange for it," how much life do we want to exchange for the services we get? It is necessary – at first – that the users are conscious of releasing data. And it is not given for granted. On the other hand, it is essential to understand how much say they have in the management once they have given the data.

The dichotomy between control and privacy then could evolve into a more complex reality based on privacy control. A reality in which the users could decide which data to release, to whom and how. They could also take advantage of these data themselves. This is platform cooperation, opposing surveillance capitalism, placing the user at the center of the process of value-making and also at the center of the model of valorization. This model replaces the process of structural control carried out by platforms with a model of cooperative management of data without leaving out the producers – the users themselves – from the valorization process. This valorization has the merit of making people perceive that the services they are using are not for free as they seem to be and promote the acquisition of awareness, a fundamental process, as the world gets more and more connected.
The platform cooperativism has another significant merit: it proved that an alternative is always possible. Even if it seems utopian, challenging to realize, or extreme.

In an economy based on data, technologies created the right conditions so that a few actors could build real empires on those data. They also laid the foundations so that the same empires rethink their development horizons, considering that the disintermediation processes enabled by technology could reduce them significantly. It is difficult to envisage a future in which platform cooperativism takes a leading role. Still, it is fundamental to imagine that it is an admonishment to remind us that technology allows disintermediating what technology itself contributed to creating.

In the balance between privacy and control, surveillance capitalism and platform cooperativism are the two opposites. To define the right blend, society is called upon making the right choices, according to which the sustainability principles must be the guide.

Openness or closure?

Security or freedom. Privacy or control. No matter if we are looking from a social, institutional, or industrial point of view, both choices lead us to the decision of envisaging the social model in its entirety: what kind of world do we want? An open-world or a closed world?

The definition of the models oriented towards security or freedom or the immolation of privacy for the need of control will depend on this choice.

Based on this choice, we will understand whether to use technology – neutral in its nature – to build bridges or walls.

The single choice dimensions – freedom or security, privacy, or control – are not independent but strictly correlated. It is of particular interest to analyze the association of these concepts beyond their individual domain of choice: for example, security is to be combined with privacy or control? And what about freedom?

The answer depends on the perspective.

From the institutions' perspective, Governments tend to consider the concept of security (of the country) linked to the control (of the citizens). In essence, the more the Government monitors its citizens, the better it can guarantee their security. This approach does not seem to be oriented towards freedom and openness ideals, but today it levers – in situations of economic, political, and social instability – on the citizens' fears and uncertainty. Fear and uncertainty always lead to narrowness. Openness towards the other, the new, the different requires change, adjustment, and cross-breeding processes. In a situation of fear, change is not the most suited option to get reassured. People tend to seek shelter in their comfort

zones, avoiding openness towards the different and the underlay challenge.
In a closed society, technologies become insidious control instruments that can enter into the citizens' lives and potentially wipe out their privacy. In this world where the users spend most of their time on the Web, controlling the Web means controlling people.

What if we stared from the citizen's point of view? The cards on the table would change, as the connections between the different concepts. In the citizen's perspective, security does not mean necessarily that a third party – even the State – can enter his life, not even for the greater good. On the contrary, security depends on the ability to guarantee privacy. We need to keep in mind that the private sphere's external invasion, even if made by the Government, is to be considered an illicit intrusion[222]. Paradoxically, each citizen's freedom is to erect a wall defending him from other people, media (social or not), and the institution's intrusions. The more technology becomes intrusive, the better it is to guarantee a private space. An "enclosed" space. But this closure is just illusory because actually, it is a closure towards control, that is to say, an openness towards freedom to keep the property of the private.

An open society can guarantee the citizens' privacy protection without renouncing this fundamental right in the name of security. A security that runs the risk of becoming a control instrument.

However, the contrast between openness and closure does not affect only the relation between Government and citizens, but also – strongly – the chosen economic model. The platforms we use every day to talk to our friends, exchange messages, do research, watch videos, and collect our data and, consequently, our preferences and intentions. In this condition, the user cannot build a tall enough wall to protect him from their omnipresence. For social network sites and research engines, we are like open books. Does this openness towards the platform economy's actors correspond to a likewise openness of the platform towards the users? Suffice

[222] S. Rodotà Tecnopolitica. La democrazia e le nuove tecnologie della comunicazione(Technopolitics. Democracy and New Communication Technologies), Editori Laterza, 2004.

to say that their business model is based, as we said[223], on the concept of *walled gardens*.

The Net is born with the concepts of freedom and openness, fundamental for its development. However, the platform economy reduced the openness level in the Web. With the platforms' supremacy, it is progressively enclosing the users within walled gardens, beautiful but also insidious for their potential effects. The platforms are the result of technological choices, that is true, but above all, they are the result of value-making models at the center of public debate: how much control over the users' information (and choices) should be permitted to a private operator, even if performing its activities?

To which extent is it possible to use data-analysis models and information structuring unknown to the users themselves?

Once again, the debate is focused on the contrast between openness and closure. In this case, we are talking about algorithms. We live in what has been called algocracy, a society regulated by the power of algorithms. It is thus crucial to understand if that algorithm is open or closed. In other terms: does the user have the right to know why certain information is kept from him and certain is displayed? Suppose what the SEO experts say is true, and the best way to hide a corpse is to put it on Google's second page. In that case, it is fundamental to understand the logic behind which data, information, or an element of knowledge are displayed or hidden. This means the algorithms' transparency (openness) or closure.
Today, these algorithms define the criteria used to index the information, manage interpersonal communication, promote products, and are – and will be – more and more present in our lives because they are used to train artificial intelligence. The artificial intelligence that contributes to job selection, the therapies for diseases, to choose a car direction and its behavior in case of incidents, to solve legal matters. In conclusion: we need to decide if the rules used to carry out most of our activities should be open and shared or closed and hidden from those who will be inevitably affected by them.

---

[223] Cf. chapter 2.

This decision is far from simple. The revenue and the growth, and consequently, the survival of enterprises depends on the algorithms (and their secrecy) and the rules they follow. Also, millions of people make choices and decisions based on the algorithm results. It will not be easy to outline the boundary between the algorithms' openness for the greater good and the closure to safeguard the competitiveness of platforms.

On the other hand, when dealing with technological choices, the comparison between open and closed business models is not recent. There is no certainty that closure will be the only way to produce benefits. In other terms, it is not assumed that to develop a functional business model in line with a sustainable economy; we need to be oriented towards trade secrets and copyright. On the contrary, many elements are suggesting otherwise. In the debate about patents as an opportunity to protect ownership, most people reckon that patents are detrimental because they stop the innovation processes and slow down development.

The first consideration is that it is impossible – from a sustainability point of view – to live in a society ruled by algorithms without sharing the rules?

We need to make another reflection: without the Web's openness, would the birth of factories based on a closure business model have been possible? We are not referring to a mere ethical or ideal dimension. We are referring to those factories that today are developing a competitive advantage starting from a closure-oriented approach that was based on an open model[224]in the first place. One of the closest technological ecosystems is Apple. In its turn, Apple operating system is based on the derivation of an operating system that it would not have developed without open models[225]. Other important actors embraced development models

---

[224] OSX is an operating system developed by Apple for its computer. It is based on a reference architecture UNIX from BSD family (Berkley software Distribution). It is the origin variation of the Unix, developed at The Berkley Univeersity, at the base of one of the major families for operating systems.

[225] The free software also allowed the birth of the licensed software. It is always distributed with a licence, guaranteeing the four fundamental freedoms (use, analysis,

based on open systems. It is the case, for example, with Google. It bases its platforms on open source and also releases products displaying their code and distributing them with open licenses. In conclusion: value-making is the result of choices, and it is not assumed that it needs to pass through approaches based on closure. These choices can be oriented towards maximizing the profit or towards sustainability models that will balance the profit – without demonizing it – with a deep reflection on the social impact we want to achieve.

In conclusion: the choices about openness and closure cross different dimensions that reconnect to the definition of our society's characteristics. The balancing is often complex and rich in contradictions, a precursor of conflicts between economic and social sustainability. This choice encompasses the whole value industry. Starting from its connotation linked to a mainly technological dimension, regarding the contrasts between closed and open source.[226]The choice then shifts to the openness of the information: the traditional model for information distribution is based on the copyright, now the new approach, which is developing side by side to first, is called copyleft[227]. The choice then moves to the way it is elaborated and distributed: in a context oriented towards social sustainability, is it possible that society ignores the very same algorithms' rules on which it is based? And is it possible that it does not codetermine them? This is of significant impact on economic models and, of course, on governance models.

Talking about the firsts, closed systems juxtapose ecosystems open to innovation: defining these dynamics' characteristics and limits will be the

---

modification and redistribution). Some licences, called copyleft impose that when redistributing the software the licence is unmodified, to guarantee the four freedom; the other licences are called non-copyleft, they provide distribution as a gift, and do not limit redistribution, allowing to have a non-copyleft software starting from a copyleft code.

[226] Often confused with free software, the open source is characterized by the openness and the release of its source code, allowing everyone to use it, study it, modify it in order to redistribute it and share it with others.

[227] Copyleft is a pun. It identifies a right-management policy based on license in which the author (the owner of the rights on the work) specifies to the users of the work (books, images, videos, music) that it can be used, spread and modified freely, respecting some essential conditions dictated by the author.

most important and challenging activity of the years to come. Today a few actors possess a lot of information about billions of users. They manage this information on the basis of closed rules, hidden from those who are both clients of the offered services (not for free) and source of the produced information (used without knowing as payment for the services). What are the conditions to make this model sustainable? What will be the action to make it sustainable?

Talking about the seconds, for years, we have been talking about data-driven governance; that is the possibility for the Government to make sensible choices on the basis of the magnitude of available data. And for years, we have been talking about open governance, which is necessary to manage countries' decisions and operating process following transparency, cooperation, and participation principles. Both these methods have shown to be mere words in most parts of the world, oriented on the building of consent over the building of innovative and efficient governance models. We find ourselves in need – at the dawning of the artificial intelligence challenge – of getting back those concepts and filling them with new meaning. This new model must open the governments to their citizens' participation, promoting the proxy principle, typical of any representative democracy. These processes do not need to go beyond this principle, in the perspective of direct utopian democracy. They need to allow people to comprehend the choices that they are contributing to make and take an active role. We have the right conditions to build cooperative and participative open governance models, but it will require – more than a technological dimension – the necessity to face a tremendous cultural challenge.

Reasoning about openness and closure from a sustainability point of view and in relation to the role of technology means to start a reflection on different grounds, beginning with the kind of society we would like to achieve. Asking ourselves what kind of society technologies will lead us to is methodologically incorrect and also dangerous: we will be driven in the cognitive tunnel in which technologies rule the game. We need to ask ourselves what kind of world we want, an open or closed world, and what we can do to achieve it, supported by digital technology.

Ownership or consumption?

For years many self-styled theorists of the new economy have lived the myth of disintermediation. This disintermediation could have brought about a radical change in our concept of economy, in commercial relations, and the management of markets. Actually, the management of markets and commercial relations have changed, but not towards disintermediation, as predicted back then. In those years, on the contrary, we experienced a process of reintermediation of the production chains. It has been made by those actors coming from the digital world. For that reason, they adopted their models for many different industries, reshaping the dynamics and the processes and thus redefining entire value chains. Apple with music, Samsung with photography, Booking.com with tourism, Amazon with commerce, Netflix with video distribution, Uber with urban transportation (the list could be longer), produced a real sense change that, starting from the digital, reshaped entire fields in the name of disintermediation.

Disintermediation refers to the elimination of some intermediaries, made useless by technologies. Reintermediation refers to a transformation of markets, in which new subjects replace the old actors. Confusion between disintermediation and reintermediation created many consequences.
In the first place, they brought about a great difficulty in framing the theme. Confusing the processes of reintermediation and disintermediation contributed to fostering the myth of sharing economy (through the usual commercial channels' disintermediation, the local producers could reach the final user, and the users themselves could enable sharing and exchange processes.) They also fed terminological and conceptual con-

fusion. Believing that the platform economy actors were enabling disintermediation processes and the sharing economy developed a warped way of approaching the sector.

It is necessary to analyze the sharing economy concept to understand its weight (and its consequences). The base conception is (apparently) simple, and it can be summarized in one question: do we need the drill or the hole it makes[228]?
The happy Italian drill-owners, almost 15 million, use it on average 30 minutes and 20 holes for its entire existence—two euros per hole. So, if every condominium had a 'shared drill' (a sort of condominium drill), the family budget expenses would be optimized, and we could have a better drill, and so on. But, you know, a man is not a man without his drill, tidily stored in his toolbox. Who cares if the hole to put a nail is as big as the English Channel? If this same example is applied to the industries and the means of production, it is clear that the weight of the matter is heavier than the ego of the italic drill-man. The small-sized Italian farming industries often possess oversized means related to practical usage. The consequence is an increase in costs and possible bankruptcy. This possibility is not enough to overcome the cultural wall blocking the sharing of the thrasher with the neighbor farm.
The idea of sharing a product or a service to optimize the costs is excellent, but its application is far from simple. There are actually many pragmatic problems: do the users share the product together or at different moments? How do they decide who can use the resource? Who makes the product available? How do the users pay? Who makes it work? Who is responsible for it? Who manages the necessary data, and who takes advantage of them? To do what? Just to name a few questions.
The sharing of a dismissed room in one's apartment or the sharing of an industrial press face the same issues, with the due differences, of course. These problems can be dealt with, thanks to Web technologies. It is not a coincidence that the sharing economy, known from the barter's time and medieval commonality in Italy's rural areas, can now find a new shape, a new place, and new meanings in the Web.

---

[228] R. Botsman, R. Rogers, What's mine is yours, the rise of collaborative economy, Harpercollins Publishers, 2010.

As it always happens, we run the risk of turning a simple matter into a complicated one. We shift from a commonality system, in which a hundred people, knowing each other, decide to share a wood oven, to a system allowing to share products with hundred of thousand strangers all over the world, and the difference is not banal. And inevitably, to follow a trend or only for ignorance, we attribute the expression sharing economy to those phenomena which have nothing to do with it. They are just perfect cases of industries' reintermediation.

An example? BlaBlaCar, a famous service allowing carpooling (the sharing of the transport costs with the car owner), has nothing to do, in methods and merits, with systems such as FreeNow or AppTaxi, used by taxi drivers.

The first one reflects a collaborative consumption system (to use Rachel Botzman's definition) of the resources that can be considered a type of sharing economy. The second one is just a digital reboot of an old service – the RadioTaxi – which has nothing to do with the sharing economy.

And again, talking about social eating[229], the platform, and the available services being equal, there are some differences in how the service is offered: occasionally sharing a dinner with friends or with strangers is way different from offering a home restaurant service every evening. In both cases, it is possible to use the same platform, but the first one is oriented towards the sharing economy, the second runs the risk of being a mere unauthorized food service.

In conclusion: recent history taught us that the internet up to now did not enable a real disintermediation process (things could change in the future), but it created new intermediaries that replaced the old ones, producing great impacts on the old operators. This process is known as "uberization," that is, a phenomenon according to which a digital operator redefines a chain's rules, replacing the old actors.

---

[229] Social eating is a phenomenon born within sharing economy. It organizes, through the digital platforms, convivial meetings (lunches or dinners) to share with strangers. Gnammo is the major Italian platform. It explains in its ethic policy that it is "an activity with the scope of organizing no-profit cooking events amongst friends, through a reservation that must be accepted by the cooker. A similar organization is Home Restaurant, but it has a business purpose. The Italian Government issued some law instruments starting from 2016, confusing the two sectors and risking to create a law disparity between the digital and the analogic channels.

Secondly, the reasoning about the sharing economy is entangled in confusion with the gig economy concept.
The sharing economy concept is well-structured, many-sided, and complex, but its basic idea is that the ownership of goods, competencies, means of production can be shared amongst different actors thanks to distributed software platforms.
The concept of the gig economy, on the other hand, is quite different. It was born in the United States, where it is a habit for young people and students to make up their money with small gigs, such as mowing the lawn or – to mention a famous activity for those who have been to the States – selling lemonades at the corner of the streets. This phenomenon was not born with the internet, and the Web did not generate it. However, the Web allowed industrializing its approach thanks to online platforms developed to put into contact supply and demand. What do the sharing economy and gig economy have in common? Nothing. Both phenomena are just using platforms to regulate and manage the relations between the parties.

The availability of regulated meeting systems for supply and demand, together with a changed context, created a significative dyscrasia: what happens when a model created in a determined economic context with determined characteristics moves to a completely different context? What happens if the gigs made by the college student at weekends become a structured source of income? What happens if the concept of occasional work becomes a dangerous substitute for flexible work? Something goes wrong.
Not only in Italy but also in the States, the expression gig economy is progressively changing. It happens then that the gigs are not made by students who want to pay for their holidays and all those who cannot find a real job. The term gig economy now describes not only occasional little works but also those jobs that cannot offer a decent safeguard for the worker, and thus are called with the diminutive term.

We are confusing the sharing economy with the gig economy, and consequently, we are ascribing to the first the problems generated by the application of platform economy models to the second. Which ones? For example, regulation issues. We need to understand if we are trying to give rules and protection to the activity of making-up money or if this activity is turning into something different. This is preparatory to understand what kind of safeguards we need to enact. It is righteous to try and safeguard the activity of delivering a single pizza, but trying to find a subordinate and dependent relation jeopardizes the sense of this model, making it unsustainable. Today, the gig economy is living in a dangerous limbo that confuses the concept of safeguard with that of stabilization.

In conclusion: the first period of the sharing economy was tormented with misunderstandings. These misunderstandings, playing with the evocative power of the matter, bent it with warped interpretations, but they have nothing to do with the shift – potentially landmark – from models based on ownership to models based on consumption.

The migration from the concept of ownership to the concept of consumption marks an essential change in the sharing economy development's point of view, even if we are far from seeing its effects (it will be interesting to observe the possible applications of the distributed ledger technologies). It is a significant change even related to the dynamics of the circular economy.[230]
Reasoning in terms of consumption rather than possession accustoms the client and the industries, the citizen, and the institutions to think about distributed ownership and – in the same way – distributed responsibilities on the managed resources.
The sharing economy is also a shared responsibility. This factor can be a kick-start for processes oriented towards a circular economy. The concept of consumption excludes, potentially, the concept of ownership and enables a path towards a real perception of shared responsibility for the products in every step of their life-cycle. In other words, the products' life can be managed regardless of who is using them in that particular moment and regardless of who produced the single components. For exam-

---

[230] With the expression circular economy, referring to the definition given by the Ellen MacArthur Foundation, we mean that economy able to regenerate itself. In a circular economy there are two kind of material fluxes: the biological flux, reintegrated in the biosphere, and the technical flux that needs to be recycled without entering the biosphere.

ple, the plastic used to make an object will keep concerning both the object and the user's producer. This can also mean that the recycling process is not only a matter of the last link of the chain. It will also encompass all the links of the chain. In this sense, the rewarding mechanisms on which the blockchain is based can be a good kick-start to support the circular economy. Rewarding, in the blockchain, is a mechanism according to which the users have benefits whenever they produce value for the community (for example, when using their computer's time, they create a new bitcoin and earn a little piece of it). If – for example – whenever we use a shared object, we earned a consumption debit (related to the consumption of the good or the CO_2 emission to produce it), that debit could be compensated with credits issuing from righteous behaviors (such as recycling correctly the waste connected to the product or producing less waste on average with the other users). Recording credits and debits in a blockchain, the user could be lured to obtain a positive balance, spendable on concrete advantages. It could be a discount on the garbage tax or a reduced price for the consumption of the services used in the perspective of consumption over ownership. The greater vision is to build virtuous paths acting on the sharing lever to support economic and environmental sustainability.

In conclusion: the choice regarding the switch from ownership models to consumption models of the products is functional to the optimization of the production costs. It also produces a lesser impact on the environment, enhancing the relationship between efficiency and efficacy. It also reduces the squanders and enables paths oriented to the support of the circular economy. That is why it is essential to contextualize the theme, draw its interpretative outlines, and support its development. We must be careful not to mistake it with the concepts of the platform economy, re-intermediation, or gig economy, which could lead to misleading and warped interpretations and could jeopardize the real opportunities sprung from a proper implementation.

Users or actors?

Networks and digital technologies have the merit of transforming people from users of a system into stakeholders able to interact with it. While thinking about how the world was like before the advent of the internet, we struggle to conceive real interaction processes on a large scale. The media ecosystem, for instance. Radio, television, and newspapers were not based – either are nowadays – on the confrontation and interaction with their users and not surprisingly defined as listeners, audience, readers. Ultimately, inactive elements of a media system are conceived to work unidirectionally. The advent of the internet has been a game-changer. User-generated content puts every single user in the position of being the protagonist in a system based on the possibility of actively express his own opinion. Forums and blogs enabled – although with different dynamics: the first based on a more community-oriented approach, the second on a Web[231]-oriented one – authentic interaction and involvement processes.

When talking about social network sites, things change drastically. They have taken to extremes the relationship dimension, at times, compromising the content. Still, they have also jeopardized the tension towards the engagement, that has represented the most important seed of change planted in the society by the Web. In the social network era, we risk that people have the feeling of playing some sort of active role in the act, whereas, in reality, they perform just the simple role of users, inactive while receiving messages as much as spreading them. On the one hand, the algorithms supposed to intercept and satisfy preferences: on the

[231] S. Epifani, A. Jacona, R. Lippi, M. Paolillo, *Manuale di Comunicazione politica in Rete*,(Manual of politics Communication on the Web) Editrice Apes, 2011.

other, phenomena such as Fake news or even more insidious deep-fake[232]undermine the basis of their awareness dimension as much as the possibility to develop real and genuine interactions. Thereby, not only do people riskì78 regress from stakeholder to users but also to experience this without even being aware that that regression took place.

It is an illusion to participate, which concerns not only social network sites but involves the whole digital ecosystem on which they are based. The platforms' solicitations – on either social media, e-commerce websites, or search engines – produce inductive situations based on dynamics gradually contrived and coercive. In these dynamics, a person's freedom risks to be just illusory. Like some sort of conditioned freedom, where algorithms progressively control actions. They could switch from foreseeing the users' behaviors to dictate their actions. It is enough to consider satellite navigation systems for cars: nowadays, they suggest the shortest journey based on the detected traffic, but won't they be the ones to determine which will be the busiest road, based on the suggested journey, when everybody uses them?

It is difficult to conceive a positive dimension based on this concept. It is not imaginable either, in such a scenario, to think in terms of social sustainability.
Nevertheless, we must consider that the instruments that might ignite those effects are the very same that allowed billions of people to connect, know each other, open their own perspectives to the world.

Once again, we are not facing a predetermined path, but a direction that will be taken downline of choice. The fate of humankind, whether they are destined to be actors in a dynamic and interactive system, rather than users in a dimension that sees them inactive while experiencing an illusory engagement, will depend on how we choose, in the next few years,

---

[232] The English expression *deepfake* intersects the expression of *deep learning* (the set of techniques that allow AI to learn and recognize shapes) with the term *fake*. The main issue is that its application allows the creation of videos in which spoken words and images caught on the web are mixed, manufacturing fake videos. They can be barely discerned from the original ones, in which protagonists appear to say and act in a way that does not reflect the reality.

to support the development of large platforms and, along with them, the features of the society that they contribute to building.

The choice of being users or actors is, ultimately, a choice that concerns awareness. Awareness that represents the core element of a decision system that humankind will have to adopt regarding the relationship between man and digital technologies and how to make them a sustainability instrument. Understanding the potential dynamics produced by technologies is fundamental to induce processes that steer the course.

From an individual point of you, assuming that using a social network site or purchasing on-line makes us "aware users," it is a risk that we cannot run.

In a complex ecosystem, like the one we live in – and we will – always more embedded, it is essential to observe the elements that made it while going beyond black boxes that take part in it, to understand the functioning, risks, and opportunities. Open black boxes[233], break them if necessary, means to understand the dynamics, defuse risks, and grab opportunities. Rejecting innovation is not how we survive the progress, but understanding its features and foster it in a way that makes it compatible with our own growth and development needs. Choosing whether to be users or actors implies choosing whether we settle for the instruments we are given, or if we want to go beyond using them, therefore understanding their nature and, depending on this, the real impact, deep and often transformative on our own reference environment.

Doing this while bearing in mind the digital sustainability entails understanding how digitalization and digital transformation might elicit a positive impact and operate so that the impact can be expressed at its best.

---

[233] In the system theory, the black box is the system's element with the unknown internal functioning. We know only the input, meaning the data that are integrated, and the output, the outcome produced by their elaboration.

A widespread awareness among users is necessary to allow them to grab the opportunities offered by these instruments without run into the hidden risks. An awareness that, from an individual level, becomes shared and social, and that from social, turns into political action.

Building a society that is aware implies on one and, build a society of actors, aware of their role and active in promoting it, and on the other hand, arrange the instruments that enable the possibility to act on a social and political level so that the individual action becomes the incentive and driving force for a collective change.

In this context, from the perspective of a sustainable future, digital technology is perhaps the most potent and available tool for humankind and the most important ally in creating a positive change.
However, humanity must understand the importance of being an active and aware actor in this change. This challenge cannot be missed. The choice of sustainability cannot exclude the proper interpretation of digital transformation dynamics and cannot exclude its contribution to determine them.

Appendix

Appendix 1: Rio Declaration on Environment and Development

1. Human beings are at the centre of concerns for sustainable development. They are entitled to a healthy and productive life in harmony with nature.
2. States have, in accordance with the Charter of the United Nations and the principles of international law, the sovereign right to exploit their own resources pursuant to their own environmental and developmental policies, and the responsibility to ensure that activities within their jurisdiction or control do not cause damage to the environment of other States or of areas beyond the limits of national jurisdiction.
3. The right to development must be fulfilled so as to equitable meet developmental and environmental needs of present and future generations.
4. In order to achieve sustainable development, environmental protection shall constitute an integral part of the development process and cannot be considered in isolation from it.
5. All States and all people shall cooperate in the essential task of eradicating poverty as an indispensable requirement for sustainable development, in order to decrease the disparities in standards of living and better meet the needs of the majority of the people of the world.
6. The special situation and needs of developing countries, particularly the least developed and those most environmentally vulnerable, shall be given special priority. International actions in the field of environment and development should also address the interests and needs of all countries.
7. States shall cooperate in a spirit of global partnership to conserve, protect and restore the health and integrity of the Earth's ecosystem. In view of the different contributions to global environmental degradation, States have common but differentiated responsibilities. The developed countries acknowledge the re-

sponsibility that they bear in the international pursuit of sustainable development in view of the pressures their societies place on the global environment and of the technologies and financial resources they command.

8. To achieve sustainable development and a higher quality of life for all people, States should reduce and eliminate unsustainable patterns of production and consumption and promote appropriate demographic policies.
9. States should cooperate to strengthen endogenous capacity-building for sustainable development by improving scientific understanding through exchanges of scientific and technological knowledge, and by enhancing the development, adaptation, diffusion and transfer of technologies, including new and innovative technologies.
10. Environmental issues are best handled with the participation of all concerned citizens, at the relevant level. At the national level, each individual shall have appropriate access to information concerning the environment that is held by public authorities, including information on hazardous materials and activities in their communities, and the opportunity to participate in decision-making processes. States shall facilitate and encourage public awareness and participation by making information widely available. Effective access to judicial and administrative proceedings, including redress and remedy, shall be provided.
11. States shall enact effective environmental legislation. Environmental standards, management objectives and priorities should reflect the environmental and developmental context to which they apply. Standards applied by some countries may be inappropriate and of unwarranted economic and social cost to other countries, in particular developing countries.
12. States should cooperate to promote a supportive and open international economic system that would lead to economic growth and sustainable development in all countries, to better address the problems of environmental degradation. Trade policy measures for environmental purposes should not constitute a means of arbitrary or unjustifiable discrimination or a disguised restriction on international trade. Unilateral actions to deal with

environmental challenges outside the jurisdiction of the importing country should be avoided. Environmental measures addressing transboundary or global environmental problems should, as far as possible, be based on an international consensus.

13. States shall develop national law regarding liability and compensation for the victims of pollution and other environmental damage. States shall also cooperate in an expeditious and more determined manner to develop further international law regarding liability and compensation for adverse effects of environmental damage caused by activities within their jurisdiction or control to areas beyond their jurisdiction.
14. States should effectively cooperate to discourage or prevent the relocation and transfer to other States of any activities and substances that cause severe environmental degradation or are found to be harmful to human health.
15. In order to protect the environment, the precautionary approach shall be widely applied by States according to their capabilities. Where there are threats of serious or irreversible damage, lack of full scientific certainty shall not be used as a reason for postponing cost-effective measures to prevent environmental degradation.
16. National authorities should endeavour to promote the internalization of environmental costs and the use of economic instruments, taking into account the approach that the polluter should, in principle, bear the cost of pollution, with due regard to the public interest and without distorting international trade and investment.
17. Environmental impact assessment, as a national instrument, shall be undertaken for proposed activities that are likely to have a significant adverse impact on the environment and are subject to a decision of a competent national authority.
18. States shall immediately notify other States of any natural disasters or other emergencies that are likely to produce sudden harmful effects on the environment of those States. Every effort shall be made by the international community to help States so afflicted.

19. States shall provide prior and timely notification and relevant information to potentially affected States on activities that may have a significant adverse transboundary environmental effect and shall consult with those States at an early stage and in good faith.
20. Women have a vital role in environmental management and development. Their full participation is therefore essential to achieve sustainable development.
21. The creativity, ideals and courage of the youth of the world should be mobilized to forge a global partnership In order to achieve sustainable development and ensure a better future for all.
22. Indigenous people and their communities, and other local communities, have a vital role in environmental management and development because of their knowledge and traditional practices. States should recognize and duly support their identity, culture and interests and enable their effective participation in the achievement of sustainable development.
23. The environment and natural resources of people under oppression, domination and occupation shall be protected.
24. Warfare is inherently destructive of sustainable development. States shall therefore respect international law providing protection for the environment in times of armed conflict and cooperate in its further development, as necessary.
25. Peace, development and environmental protection are interdependent and indivisible.
26. States shall resolve all their environmental disputes peacefully and by appropriate means in accordance with the Charter of the United Nations.
27. States and people shall cooperate in good faith and in a spirit of partnership in the fulfillment of the principles embodied in this Declaration and in the further development of international law in the field of sustainable development.

Appendix 2: Millennium Development Goals

1: ERADICATE EXTREME POVERTY & HUNGER
Halve the proportion of people whose income is less than $1.25 a day

2: ACHIEVE UNIVERSAL PRIMARY EDUCATION
Ensure that children everywhere, boys and girls alike, will be able to complete a full course of primary schooling

3: PROMOTE GENDER EQUALITY AND EMPOWER WOMEN
Eliminate gender disparity in primary and secondary education and in all levels of education no later than 2015

4: REDUCE CHILD MORTALITY
Reduce by two thirds the under-five mortality rate

5: IMPROVE MATERNAL HEALTH
Reduce by three quarters the maternal mortality ratio

6: COMBAT HIV/AIDS, MALARIA AND OTHER DISEASES
Have halted and begun to reverse the spread of HIV/AIDS

7: ENSURE ENVIRONMENTAL SUSTAINABILITY
Integrate the principles of sustainable development into country policies and programmes and reverse the loss of environmental resources. Halve the proportion of the population without sustainable access to safe drinking water and basic sanitation

8: DEVELOP A GLOBAL PARTNERSHIP FOR DEVELOPMENT
Develop further an open, rule-based, predictable, non-discriminatory trading and financial system. Address the special needs of least developed countries

Appendix 3: The 2030 Agenda

1. No poverty: end extreme poverty in all forms by 2030.
2. Zero hunger: end hunger, achieve food security and improved nutrition and promote sustainable agriculture
3. Good health and well-being: ensure healthy lives and promote well-being for all at all ages
4. Quality education: ensure inclusive and equitable quality education and promote lifelong learning opportunities for all
5. Gender equality: achieve gender equality and empower all women and girls
6. Clean water and sanitation: ensure availability and sustainable management of water and sanitation for all
7. Affordable and clean energy: ensure access to affordable, reliable, sustainable and modern energy for all
8. Decent work and economic growth: promote sustained, inclusive and sustainable economic growth, full and productive employment and decent work for all
9. Industry innovation and infrastructure: build resilient infrastructure, promote inclusive and sustainable industrialization and foster innovation
10. reduced inequalities: reduce inequality within and among countries
11. sustainable cities and communities: make cities and human settlements inclusive, safe, resilient and sustainable
12. responsible consumption an dproduction: ensure sustainable consumption and production patterns
13. climate action: take urgent action to combat climate change and its impacts
14. life below water: conserve and sustainably use the oceans, seas and marine resources for sustainable development
15. life on land: protect, restore and promote sustainable use of terrestrial ecosystems, sustainably manage forests, combat desertification, and halt and reverse land degradation and halt biodiversity loss

16. peace, justice and strong institutions: promote peaceful and inclusive societies for sustainable development, provide access to justice for all and build effective, accountable and inclusive institutions at all levels
17. strengthen the means of implementation and revitalize the global partnership for sustainable development

Appendix 4: Digital Sustainability Manifesto

1. The digital transformation does not just affect processes, changing the way of doing things. It reaches their deep nature, redefining the purpose.
2. The digital transformation develops changes on people, environment, society, culture and economy. It is a common responsibility to contribute in the definition of the direction of the above changes.
3. Technology developments can only be partially oriented or determined. Any attempt to understand the dynamics of the digital transformation, and to influence them, must start from this assumption.
4. Defining the role of digital in society passes through two elements: the direction embedded into technologies' developments and the feedback produced by these, on people, economy, and environment during the changing process of society itself. Those elements are indissolubly linked and profoundly interdependent.
5. Restrict ourselves to question if technology is "good" or "bad" is pointless. Technology is neither good nor bad. However, this does not exclude that it produces effects in either direction. It is fundamental to question ourselves on the negative effects, to minimize them, and on the positive ones, to enhance them.
6. The greatest task for humankind is to understand how technology can be functional, not the contrary. To achieve this, we should try to direct its development so that technology can produce, in a utilitarian view, positive effects on society.
7. The concept of positive effect on society is actualized by the technology's contribution to the development of a sustainable society.
8. Economic, social and environmental sustainability criteria, as defined by the United Nations and consolidated in Agenda 2030, must be a beacon of inspiration in the choices which will determine the development of technologies as tools to build a sustainable future.
9. The cultural system made up of intellectuals, academics, researchers, and information professionals must promote the

knowledge of the technologic tool while promoting the development of widespread awareness among citizens, institutions, businesses, and decision-makers.

10. History shows how technology has improved living conditions. The conduct of decision-makers must be oriented to nurture the greatest technological development in an interpretive context, which – without slowing down the progress – should steer it in a direction compatible and functional to a sustainable world.

Appendix 5: *Fake News* Manifesto

1. Fake news issue has always existed: nowadays it feeds on new dynamics

News that is deliberately fake or artificially altered has been intentionally fabricated and diffused since forever. Fake news is now a relevant topic as web platforms, and social media remove any mediation and make filters, controls, professional, and ethical rules of the traditional editorial systems, totally ineffective. Networks start deconstruction processes in the information system; they disempower the centralized models and create new instant informative ecosystems, permeable, and always more user-generated. The conversational arena, once segmented according to the control of complex codes, lose their identity and context. Everyone has access to a single conversational/dialogic context, produced by the interaction between equals and subject only to specific platform mechanisms: algorithms and policy. This has determined great opportunities for expression and debate but also great risks.

2. The generative dynamic of Social Media is accentuated by the crisis of the role held by science in the post-truth era.

The Fake News phenomenon is accentuated by the gradual loss of faith in those systems supposed to "manage" the scientific knowledge and to have the final say on what is true or false.

In a context where everyone talks about everything, the emotional dimension linked to a fact overcomes the factual one. What leads the users to share an "a-scientific" position or endorsing "alternative scientific" methods (such as no-vax and chemical trails) is the emotional affinity among equals, in the first case, or mistrust in the scientific methods, which is associated with the rhetoric of a compromised science with specific interests. Social networks focused on the individual offer a conversational plot in which condition/consequence becomes an individual claim, which overpowers any rational and valid reasoning.

3. The immediacy of sharing overcomes the necessity of thought

The rapidity of communications voids the reflection and the emotional detachment permitted by traditional media, replacing the thought process with the "instant sharing." Being absorbed in a social environment of dialogue and commonality prevents the emotional "cooling down" and instead intensifies an immediate "heating up" of the response and the desire of being promptly present in the exchange that takes place: sharing comes before the in-depth analysis.

4. Censorship is not only against the nature and structure of the network but also ineffective

The open and adaptive nature of the network prevents any censorship since it is unethical in relation to the structural dimensions (epistemic, morphological, and topological), resulting in ineffective attempts.
In relation to Fake News, there is no "new felony" to regulate. Laws that determine the dynamics already regulate each juridical relevant aspect. The concept of controlling in a specific and exclusive way the digital dimension by creating a double normative binary will create an unacceptable asymmetry, even more, if we consider that the entity that controls the generative dynamic of Social Network Site might be taken into account.

5. The censorship of Fake News not only will be ineffective, but dangerous for the same user that is meant to protect

Entrust the platforms with the task of "auditors" of Fake News is not only useless but also risky. In a context where the information structure is already deeply dependent on the stakeholders of the platform society and on the algorithms that determine its structure and dynamic, it will bestow the power of monitoring the truth upon a system of players that hold great power.

6. Who generates Fake News is held responsible, but so is who shares them

In a network, the value of the arches (connections) is staggering compared to the hubs 'one. From the moment the memetic element of Fake News develops (in relation to the outreach) from the hub into the several connections it establishes, the responsibility of the impact of the Fake News is shared between the user which creates the arches (sharing) and the initiation of the hub itself (the maker of the original fake). A paradoxical condition then occurs, where the joint liability of spreading the fake news all over the network becomes as important as the original act of manufacturing a piece of fake information.

7. First of all, Fake News is a business

We should avoid the erroneous assumption that everything is attributable to a conspiracy: although in some instances, Fake News is spread according to propaganda or conspiracy purposes, the economic dimension is often predominant over the others. Fake News generate an economic value, which is proportionally linked to the viral transmission and the memetic coefficient of the contents they disseminate.

8. Whichever the technical solution proposed, reporting is always preferable to censorship

Regardless of the identification process of the potential Fake News, the outcome should not be immediately censorial. Any resolution should be based on reporting and alert mechanisms that tell the user that he is facing potential insidious information. This triggers a joint responsibility dynamic in the awareness of sharing, highlighting the active role of the user. Thereby, not only we rationally reduce the speed of dissemination of Fake News, but also we contribute to building a reflective exercise – individual and collective – which is based and promotes users' awareness.

9. Any control mechanism of Fake News should be based on transparent, open and iterative dynamics

The generative system that led to the decision to report news should be transparent and verifiable from third parties so that we can operate through iterative ways, which can redefine, if necessary or appropriate, such decision, enhancing cooperation and collective intelligence and creating positive externalities. In such a mechanism, the platforms are not overwhelmed with responsibilities that they should not be concerned with nor can have, but we bestow upon them the strategic role of debate enablers and warrantors of the process in an unbiased position in relation to the topics.

10. A single regulation will not overcome the problem. We need users with culture, education, and awareness

As in the case of *hatespeech*, with which it shares numerous elements, the relevance of the Fake News phenomenon is inversely proportional to the awareness level of users (digital literacy), compared to the informatics ecosystem in which they exist. The solution to the problem is mostly cultural. It abides by an awareness level from the users, whose acquisition relies on the involvement of numerous elements: from the scholar and educational system to the public debate, propriety, and sense of civic duty of the stakeholders that take part in it.

The platforms cannot turn themselves in censors on the governmental mandate: they should actively promote the development of the competencies and the respect and involvement culture, essential to exercise the right of digital citizenship of the users.

Bibliography

- AA. VV. DG Regional and Urban Policies, Guide to Social Innovation, (2013).
- AA. VV., Draft new Report ITU-R M.[IMT-2020.TECH PERF REQ] - Minimum requirements related to technical performance for IMT-2020 radio interface(s), ITU public document, (2017).
- AA. VV., Election cybersecurity: challenges and opportunities, European Union Agency for Network and Information Security - ENISA, (2019).
- AA. VV., Le crisi finanziarie nella storia, approfondimento della Consob – Commissione Nazionale per le Società e la Borsa, Autorità italiana per la vigilanza dei mercati finanziari.
- AA. VV., Our Common Future, Commissione mondiale per l'ambiente e lo sviluppo, Programma delle Nazioni Unite per l'Ambiente, (1987).
- AA. VV., Relazione sulla ricerca e l'innovazione in Italia, Consiglio Nazionale delle Ricerche, giugno 2018.
- AA. VV., The future of food and agriculture, trends and challenges, FAO, (2017).
- AA. VV., World Summit on the Information Society. Declaration of Principles. Building the Information Society: a global challenge in the new millennium, United Nations – ITU, Ginevra, 2003.
- AA.VV., Oslo Manual, Guidelines for Collecting and Interpreting Innovation Data, OCSE, (2018).
- AA. VV. DESI (Digital Economy and Society Index), Indice di digitalizzazione dell'economia e della società, Relazione nazionale, Italia, (2019).
- Aghion P., Alesina A. F., Trebbi F., Democracy, technology, and growth, Working paper, Department of Economics, Harvard University, (2007).
- Allen C., The Path to Self-Sovereign Identity, www.lifewithalacrity.com, 25 Aprile 2016.
- Aneesh A., Virtual Migration, Duke University Press, (2006).
- Angelopoulos A. N., Ameri H., Mitra D., Humayun M.. Enhanced Depth Navigation Through Augmented Reality Depth Mapping in Patients with Low Vision, Nature, (2019).
- Argyris C., Schön D.A., Organizational Learning: A Theory of Action Perspective, Addison-Wesley Pub. Co., (1978).
- Baregheh A., Rowley J., Sambrook S., Towards a multidisciplinary definition of innovation, Management decision 47.8 (2009): 1323-1339.

- Belvaux B., The Development of Social Media: Proposal for a Diffusion Model Incorporating Network Externalities in a Competitive Environment, Recherche et Applications en Marketing, (2011).
- Bentivegna S., Boccia Artieri G., Le teorie della comunicazione di massa e la sfida digitale, Editori Laterza, (2019).
- Boccia Artieri G., Stati di connessione. Pubblici, cittadini e consumatori nella (Social) Network Society, Franco Angeli, (2012).
- Bolter J., Grusin R., Remediation. Competizione e integrazione tra media vecchi e nuovi, Guerini e Associati, (2003).
- Botsman R., Rogers R., What's mine is yours, the rise of collaborative economy, Harpercollins Publishers, (2010).
- Breiman L., Statistical Modeling: The Two Cultures, Statistical Science, Institute of Mathematical Statistics, August-2001, vol. 16, n. 3, pp. 199-215.
- Briscoe G., De Wilde P., Digital Ecosystems: Evolving Service-Oriented architectures, BIONETICS 2006, Proceeding of the 1st international conference on Bio inspired models of network, information and computing system, ACM Press, (2006).
- Bruns A., Owning Is the New Sharing, Shareable, (2014).
- Capaccioli S., Criptovalute e bitcoin: un'analisi giuridica, Giuffrè Editore, (2015).
- Cerf V. G., *Internet* Access Is Not a Human Right, New York Times, January 24th, 2002.
- Chesbrough H., Open Innovation: The New Imperative for Creating and Profiting from Technology, Harward *Business* School Press, (2003).
- Christensen C., Bower J., Disruptive Technologies: catching the wave, Harward *Business* Review, (1995).
- Ciofalo G., Homo communicans. Una specie di/in evoluzione, Armando Editore, (2013).
- Comunello F., Networked sociability: riflessioni e analisi sulle relazioni sociali (anche) mediate dalle tecnologie, Guerini Scientifica, (2010).
- Costanza R., Ecological Economics: The Science and Management of Sustainability, Columbia University Press, (1991).
- Epifani S., *Business* Community, gestire il Capitale Intellettuale nella Net Economy, Franco Angeli, (2003).
- Epifani S., Farsagli S., L'innovazione come leva di crescita: il punto di vista degli imprenditori, Digital Transformation Institute - Confcommercio, (2018).
- Epifani S., Jacona A., Lippi R., Paolillo M., Manuale di Comunicazione politica in Rete, Editrice Apes, (2011).
- Freeman C., The Economics of Industrial Innovation, Penguin Modern Economic Texts, (1974).
- Gershenfeld N., Quando le cose iniziano a pensare, Garzanti, (2000).

- Gillespie T., The Politics of Platform, New Media & Society, May-2010.
- Hagel III J., The New Infomediaries, The McKinsey Quarterly, Autumn 1997, p. 54 et ss.
- Hunicke R., Le Blanc M., Zubek R., MDA: A Formal Approach to Game Design and Game Research, Northwestern University, (2004).
- Jaeggi R., Forme di vita e capitalismo, Rosenberg & Sellier, (2016).
- Jenkins H., Cultura Convergente, Maggioli Editore, (2007).
- Jongbloed B., Vossensteyn H., Access and Expansion Post-Massification: Opportunities and Barriers to Further Growth in Higher Education Participation, Routledge, (2016).
- Kumar S., Shah N., False Information on Web and Social Media: A Survey, 1-1, aprile 2018.
- Kurz R., Le crepe del capitalismo, Bepress, (2015).
- Latouche S., La scommessa della decrescita, Feltrinelli, (2007).
- Laudonio M., Panarari M., Alfabeto Grillo, Dizionario critico ragionato del Movimento 5 stelle, Mimesis, 2014
- Macey J., Sisodia R., Conscious Capitalism: Liberating the Heroic Spirit of *Business*, Harward *Business* Review Press, (2014).
- Marinelli A., Connessioni. Nuovi Media, nuove relazioni sociali, Guerini Editore, (2005).
- Marx K., Il Capitale, (1867).
- Masood E., The Great Invention: The Story of GDP and the Making and Unmaking of the Modern World, Pegasus Book, (2016).
- Maturana R.H., Varela F. G., Uribe R., Autopoiesis: the Organization of Living Systems, its Characterization and a Model, Biosystems, May-1974, vol. 5, p. 187-196.
- Moazed A., Johnson N. L., Modern Monopolies: What It Takes to Dominate the 21st-Century Economy, St. Martin's Press, (2016).
- Morozov E., The Net Delusion: The Dark Side of *Internet* Freedom, Public Affairs, (2011).
- Murphie A., Potts J., Culture and Technology, Palgrave Macmillan, (2003).
- Orwell G., 1984, Secker & Warburg, London, (1948).
- Pallante M., La decrescita felice. La qualità della vita non dipende dal PIL, Editori Riuniti, (2007).
- Parisier E., The Filter Bubble: What The *Internet* Is Hiding From You, Penguin Books Limited, (2011).
- Pearce D. W., Atkinson G. D., Capital theory and the measurement of sustainable development: an indicator of "weak" sustainability, Elsevier Science B.V, Ecological Economics, vol. 8, Ottobre 1993, p. 103-108.
- Radfar C., Bias In AI: A problem recognized but still unresolved, TechCrunch, (2019).

- Riccio L., Un tweet non fa primavera. Il ruolo dei social media nella primavera araba, Dialoghi Mediterranei, (2017).
- Rifkin J., L'Era Dell'Accesso. La rivoluzione della new economy, trad. Paolo Canton, Oscar Mondadori, (2001).
- Rodotà S., Tecnopolitica. La tecnologia e le nuove tecnologie della comunicazione, Editori Laterza, (2004).
- Roesling H., Factfulness. Dieci ragioni per cui non capiamo il mondo. E perché le cose vanno meglio di come pensiamo, Rizzoli, (2018).
- Ross A., Il nostro futuro, Feltrinelli, (2016).
- Scholz T., Platform Cooperativism: Challenging the Corporate Sharing Economy, Rosa Luxemburg Stiftung, (2016).
- Schumpeter J. A., Capitalismo, socialismo e democrazia, ETAS, (2001).
- Schwab K., The Fourth Industrial Revolution, World Economic Forum, (2015), trad. It.: La quarta rivoluzione industriale, Franco Angeli, (2016).
- Shapiro C., Information rules: a strategic guide to the network economy, Harvard *Business* Press, (1999).
- Shirky C., Here Comes Everybody, the power of organizing without organizations, Penguin Press, (2008).
- Smorto G., Le regole del Gioco del Platform Cooperativism, Impresa Sociale, (2016).
- Solow R. M., On the intergenerational allocation of natural resources, The Scandinavian Journal of Economics, March-1986, vol. 88, p. 141-149.
- Srnicek N., Platform Capitalism, Polity Books, Cambridge, (2016).
- Swhab K., The Fourth Industrial Revolution, Feltrinelli, (2019).
- Tanzi V., Le condizioni economiche e sociali in Italia intorno al 1861, Rubettino Editore, (2013).
- Taylor F. W., L'organizzazione scientifica del lavoro, Etas Kompass, (1967).
- Turner K. R., Pearce D. W., Bateman I., Economia ambientale, Il Mulino, (2003).
- Van Dijck J., Poell T., de Waal M., Platform Society: Public Values in a Connective World, Oxford University Press, (2018).
- Weber M., L'etica Protestante e lo spirito del Capitalismo, Biblioteca Universale Rizzoli, (1991).
- Zuboff S., The age of surveillance capitalism. The fight for a human future at the new frontier of power, Profile Books Ltd, (2019).

Digital Transformation Institute Foundation

http://www.digitaltransformationinstitute.it

The Digital Transformation Institute is a research institute aimed at studying the dynamics of the "sense revolution" caused by digital transformation and its contribution to economic, social, and environmental sustainability.
With a multidisciplinary approach, the Digital Transformation Institute provides readings and interpretations of the digital transformation; it offers strategic indications to the policy-makers, it intercepts the change trends and analyzes the impacts, with particular attention on how to use technologies to support sustainable development.
The Institute is a meeting point for the experts coming from the academic and research world, public and private institutions, and enterprises.
With the work Digital Sustainability, the Digital Transformation Institute launches its editorial series.

Tech economy 2030

http://www.techeconomy2030.it

Tech Economy 2030 is the first Italian online magazine devoted to digital sustainability. It was born from the merging of Tech Economy's experiences (Tech Economy is an adventure undertaken in 2012, as one of the first editorial ventures dedicated to the networked economy) and the Digital Transformation Institute. Tech Economy 2030 works in partnership with an international network made of more than 100 experts, researches, journalists, and professionals in the field.

www.ingramcontent.com/pod-product-compliance
Ingram Content Group UK Ltd.
Pitfield, Milton Keynes, MK11 3LW, UK
UKHW022026190726
13853UKWH00005B/2133

9 788894 484151